Mending a Heart

A Journey Through Open-Heart Surgery

Lynn Miclea

MENDING A HEART

A Journey Through Open-Heart Surgery

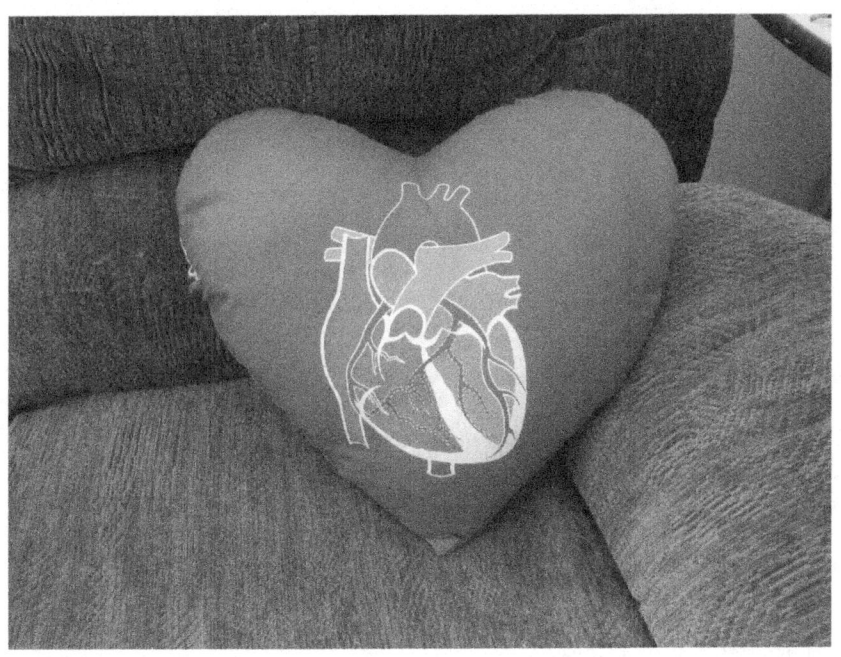

LYNN MICLEA

Copyright © 2016 Lynn Miclea

All rights reserved. No part of this publication may be reproduced or transmitted in any form or by any means, electronic or mechanical, including photocopying, recording, or by any information storage and retrieval system, without permission in writing from the author. Reviewers may quote brief passages.

ISBN-10: 1539541029
ISBN-13: 978-1539541028
CreateSpace Independent Publishing Platform
North Charleston, South Carolina

Cover photo from Morguefile.com

DEDICATION

Dedicated with much love to my amazing husband for his extraordinary love, support, and kindness through such difficult and trying situations. This book is for you, the man who pushed me to get the help I needed, was at my side every moment possible, who helped me every step of the way, and who helped me heal on so many levels.

Thank you for always being there, as my husband, nursemaid, confidant, and best friend. Thank you for all the countless ways that you helped me without any complaint, through all the medical struggles and all my self-doubts — I could not have made it without you. And thank you for continually giving me so many reasons to go on living. I am so very grateful, and I love you forever. You are my special angel here on earth.

Table of Contents

Introduction	9
Chapter 1 – Enjoying Life	13
Chapter 2 – Debilitating Weakness	19
Chapter 3 – Preliminary Diagnosis	25
Chapter 4 – Going to Maui	29
Chapter 5 – Kayak Tour	33
Chapter 6 – Difficulty Walking	39
Chapter 7 – The Echocardiogram	43
Chapter 8 – Going Downhill	49
Chapter 9 – Open-Heart Surgery	57
Chapter 10 – Recovery in the ICU	61
Chapter 11 – Competition and Exercises	69
Chapter 12 – Going Home	75
Chapter 13 – The First Shower	81
Chapter 14 – Sneezes and Visitors	87
Chapter 15 – Milestones	93
Chapter 16 – Driving	99
Chapter 17 – Cardiac Rehab	105
Chapter 18 – Returning to Routines	111
Chapter 19 – Chicago	117
Chapter 20 – Niagara Falls	121
Chapter 21 – Enjoying Life Again	125
Chapter 22 – A Poem of Gratitude	129
Epilogue	133
About the Author	139
Books by Lynn Miclea	141

Introduction

To this day, when I think back over what had happened, I am often shocked that I did not die in 2005.

Throughout my life, I had always been healthy and active. I often participated in many sports, including tennis, ping pong, swimming, hiking, skiing, canoeing, and kayaking.

When I started having problems with weakness, diminished energy, and profound shortness of breath, I tended to dismiss my symptoms as being related to either my age or being overweight and out of shape. As far as I knew, heart disease did not run in our family, so I did not consider that this could be a serious medical issue. However, as I later found out, I had severe aortic stenosis.

Aortic stenosis is one of the most common and most serious heart valve problems. Normal, healthy heart valves are thin membranes which continuously open and close in order to regulate the flow of blood through the chambers of the heart.

Blood naturally flows from the left ventricle, the lower left chamber of the heart, into the aorta, which is the main artery that supplies oxygenated blood to the body. In aortic stenosis, there is a narrowing of the aortic valve, which means that the valve does not open fully or function properly. The valve gets stiff and stays constricted, so that not enough oxygenated blood is supplied to the body.

In addition, if the valve opening is almost closed, the heart must work harder to try to pump blood through the narrow, defective valve, which can cause pressure to build up in the left ventricle. This can then thicken the heart muscle, and the heart may appear enlarged. This can ultimately lead to heart failure and death.

Aortic stenosis can be caused by calcium build-up on the valve, rheumatic fever, or a congenital heart defect. One of the most common heart defects that cause aortic stenosis is a bicuspid valve.

A normal aortic valve has three cusps, or leaflets, which open and close to control the flow of blood. A bicuspid valve has only two cusps, and this condition occurs in roughly 1% to 2% of the population, most commonly in males.

Aortic stenosis occurs more often in men than in women, and usually occurs after age 60, with symptoms often not appearing until after age 70. Roughly 2% to 5% of people over age 65 will have aortic stenosis.

A healthy aortic valve is usually open about 3.0-4.0 cm^2. As stenosis progresses, the opening gradually closes.

For reference, here is a chart showing the ranges for the aortic valve opening.

Normal aortic valve	3.0-4.0 cm^2
Mild stenosis	1.5-2.0 cm^2
Moderate	1.0-1.5 cm^2
Severe	0.8-1.0 cm^2
Critical	<0.7 cm^2

The most effective way to test for and diagnose aortic stenosis is with an echocardiogram, which is basically an ultrasound for the heart. In an echocardiogram, images are visible on a screen, and you can see the movement and functioning of the heart valves, and therefore be able to detect if any valve is not functioning properly.

For treatment of severe stenosis, valve replacement is the only option. If left untreated, this condition is fatal.

Throughout this book, in order to protect the privacy of the physicians involved, the names of the doctors have been changed.

For anyone who has any symptoms that are troubling or abnormal for you, please go to a doctor. And if you are not satisfied with that doctor's care, please seek another opinion. Your health is important, and we should not so easily dismiss atypical or troubling symptoms.

My heart goes out to anyone and any family that is touched by illness and medical issues. May you find your way to good health and deep peace.

1

Enjoying Life

"Oh my God, I can't keep going," I cried out, huffing and puffing, while laboriously trudging up the hill.

"Just a little more, we're almost there," the hike leader responded, smiling back at me over his shoulder.

"Ack! I'm already dying," I answered, feeling hot, sweaty, and exhausted.

Dumitru, hiking next to me, pointed to a shady spot under a nearby tree.

"Lynn, do you want a quick break?" he asked me, clearly not out of breath.

"Why aren't you even breathing hard?" I asked him, panting between each word.

He laughed, and I followed him into the shade. Removing his backpack, he took out two bottles of water, and handed one to me.

My body relaxed and my breathing slowed down, as I gratefully drank the cool, refreshing water. After resting in the shade a few more minutes, we then rejoined our group, which was still hiking up the hill.

It was 2002, and both of us loved these hikes up in the hills with the Sierra Club. Even when I struggled to keep up, it was still fun and invigorating, and I always felt so good afterward.

I glanced at Dumitru – my hiking buddy, my best friend, and my husband of seven years. He was in great shape, and these hikes seemed to be so easy for him.

"Want me to push you?" Dumitru asked me playfully.

"Yes, please," I answered, thankful for the help. I slowed down while he got behind me and started pushing. As the hill was steep at that point, his pushing made it much easier, and we continued hiking up the trail with our group.

A few minutes later we reached the top, and we saw that the leader was unpacking some snacks and placing them on a flat rock. Finding a shady spot, we sat down on a nearby rock, drinking our water.

"Help yourselves," the leader called out, spreading out bags of chips and cookies.

"How far did we hike?" I asked the leader, while grabbing a pack of chocolate chip cookies to share with my husband.

"This hike was three miles up, with a 1,200-foot gain, and it was fairly steep in places," he explained. "You did great. We'll be going down a different path on the way back, which will curve around and then connect back to our original path close to where we started. So the hike will be about six miles total."

"Okay, thank you," I said, as I returned to my husband with the bag of cookies.

"Three miles one way, six miles total, 1,200-foot gain," I told him, summing it up.

"That's why you're out of breath."

"So why aren't you?"

Dumitru just laughed.

Having met in the Sierra Club over ten years earlier, we had gone on many hikes, camping trips, ski trips, and canoe trips together. Our favorite times were when we were active and outside in the fresh air.

In Southern California, the weather stayed mild through all the seasons, and we could take part in outdoor activities all year long. That was one of the many reasons why we loved living in the Los Angeles area.

Looking around at the beautiful views of trees, mountains, and the Pacific Ocean in the distance, we sat there at the peak of the hill, happily munching our cookies. It was incredibly peaceful up there, and I took a deep breath, letting it out slowly.

The leader started packing up. We drank more water, and then we followed the leader on the trail back down. What a beautiful day to hike in the great outdoors, surrounded by trees, streams, nature, fresh air, and good friends. It felt almost effortless as we started down the dirt path.

Going downhill was much easier, and we talked with some of our friends on the three-mile trek through the trees, back to our car.

"That was a great hike today," I told Dumitru after we had gotten home.

"That was fun," he agreed. "Is there another hike next weekend?"

Getting out our hiking schedule, I looked at what was posted for the next weekend.

"Yes, look, there are two hikes," I answered, showing him the booklet.

Reviewing the 2002 schedule together, we circled the hikes and activities that we wanted to attend. We loved our friends in the Sierra Club, and there were always so many fun and interesting things to do with them.

In addition to hiking, we were looking forward to a camping trip and a white-water rafting trip that we had scheduled for later that year.

Over the next few years, we started scaling back on our activities. We tended to go on smaller hikes that were not quite as long or strenuous, and we went less often. That seemed to work out fine for both of us, as the demands on our time had seemed to increase.

One evening in June 2004, we went out for a scrumptious dinner at our favorite Chinese restaurant.

"What do you want to do for our anniversary next year?" Dumitru asked me between bites of almond chicken.

"Hmmm – our ten-year anniversary. That's a big one. We should do something special."

"Let's go to Hawaii," he suggested.

"That would be amazing," I answered, swallowing a tender piece of shrimp. "How about Maui? I'd love to go to Maui." I smiled at him, getting excited.

"Okay, Maui it is. And I want to go kayaking," Dumitru said.

"And snorkeling," I added enthusiastically.

As soon we got back home, I went to the computer and logged on to do research and start planning our vacation.

Researching all the activities in Maui was exciting. Our trip there next May would be so much fun.

2

Debilitating Weakness

"Let's go for a walk," Dumitru suggested to me one warm Saturday evening in early March 2005.

"Okay," I answered after a short hesitation. Over the past ten years, since we had moved into our house, we had often enjoyed leisurely strolls in our quiet residential neighborhood.

"Lynn, is something wrong? You don't feel up to it?" My husband looked at me, concern in his voice, as he noticed my hesitation.

"Well, maybe a short walk," I answered a bit reluctantly.

"Are you not feeling well?" Dumitru looked at me, his eyes filled with worry.

"I'm okay, I guess. I just can't walk very fast or very far," I explained. "I get winded easily."

"We can go slow," he answered.

We both knew that this was not normal. After all our years together going on Sierra Club hikes, not being able to casually walk around the neighborhood was unusual for me, to say the least.

"I'm sorry," I told him, trying to explain it. "I think I'm just getting too old and too out of shape." I shrugged at him, hoping he would accept that and let it go.

"We'll go as slow as you want, and we can come back whenever you need to. Sound good?" he asked me.

"Sounds good," I answered, smiling at him.

Leaving the house, we started comfortably strolling up the street. The air felt soft and warm, and a light, fresh breeze rustled the leaves overhead in the tall trees lining the street.

Half-way up the first street, I found myself already out of breath. I pulled on Dumitru's arm, huffing and puffing.

"Wait," I implored, breathing hard. "I can't walk this fast."

"This is too fast?" He looked at me, surprised. "Okay, we can walk slower. You set the pace," he offered.

I slowed down, easing back to barely a shuffle.

"This is as fast as I can walk," I said, out of breath.

"We're barely moving."

"I know. Maybe I'm just too overweight."

He squeezed my hand, but did not answer. We continued walking, very slowly, around one short block, and I held tightly to Dumitru's hand the whole way.

By the time we got back home, I felt a little dizzy and light-headed.

"Are you okay?" he asked me.

"I just need to sit down. I don't feel so good," I told him.

"Maybe you should see a doctor," he suggested.

"I'm okay. We'll see."

The rest of that weekend I rested and tried not to exert myself. Without any physical activity or exertion, I was fine and there was no problem.

On Sunday afternoon I sat down and meditated, as I had done on and off for years, hoping some deep relaxation or calmness would help.

Returning to work on Monday, I felt relieved. Much of my job consisted of sitting at my desk in the reception area of a publishing company which sold advertising copy. My duties were mostly answering phones, greeting the occasional visitor, and managing the office's accounts receivables, which included billing, collections, bank deposits, and preparation and analysis of various reports. Most of my work was on the computer, and I liked the routines and my work.

One of my duties included walking roughly 50 feet down two hallways to retrieve our company's mail from one of six mailboxes, and then bringing the mail back to my desk for sorting.

Just after 10:00 A.M., I walked the length of the two hallways to the mailbox. However, the mail had not yet been delivered, and I found the mailbox empty. Returning to my desk empty-handed, I figured that I would try again in another hour.

Sitting down at my desk after that short walk, I felt vaguely weak and light-headed. *What was wrong? Could it be my age? At 51 years old, I was not really that old, was I? Was I that out of shape?*

Maybe I am just too stressed, I thought. I took some deep breaths and tried to relax. After about ten minutes, I felt better and quickly dismissed the experience as just not feeling that well. After all, I had worked there and retrieved the mail for a few years, and I had never had a problem before.

Roughly an hour later, feeling fine and forgetting the previous weakness, I jumped up and briskly walked to the mailbox. Suddenly seriously winded, with an intense pressure building in my body, I retrieved the mail, and I slowly returned to my desk.

By the time I sat down in my chair, I was light-headed and feeling sick. Overcome with dizziness and weakness, I quickly lay down on the floor underneath my desk, worried that I might pass out. Feeling my body break out in a sweat, I lay there, weak and depleted of energy, hoping nobody would come by or need something from me. After about 15 minutes, I stopped sweating and felt my strength begin to return.

Once my equilibrium returned to normal and I felt strong enough, I got up from the floor and sat in my chair. Embarrassed, I was glad that no one had come into the reception area and seen me. With my strength back somewhat, I returned to my job duties, quickly forgetting the feelings of weakness. Easily getting lost in the collections reports, the time passed quickly.

For the rest of that week, I made sure that I walked very slowly back and forth to the mailbox. Although feeling weak and out of breath each time, it was not that bad when I took my time.

On Wednesday of the following week, our sales manager called all the employees together for a meeting. After announcing how pleased he was at our increased sales and revenue, he said he wanted all of us to relax, play a game, and have some fun.

He arranged the twelve of us in a small circle, and he then threw a few brightly-colored balloons into the group. "Try to hit the balloons to each other and not let any of them hit the floor," he told us.

Excited and laughing, we started swatting at the balloons, sending them back and forth across the circle. Being a silly, fun-loving kid at heart, I absolutely loved this. I eagerly jumped forward, hitting the balloons, gleefully laughing. After swatting at another balloon near me, I suddenly felt an awful pressure fill me.

Unable to get a full breath, I froze in place, not knowing what was wrong. I felt dizzy and sickeningly weak, wasted, and depleted of energy. I could barely move or breathe. Something was horribly wrong.

Leaving the circle of happy employees, I quickly returned to my desk in the reception area. I sat in my chair, but the intense weakness and inability to breathe persisted. Even more than simply out of breath, my entire body felt weak, sick, and terribly drained. I sat there a few minutes, trying to breathe, hoping to regain my strength.

Not feeling better, and afraid that I would pass out, I lay down on the floor under my desk, and broke out in a sweat. This had now happened a few times, but today was by far the worst. *What could be wrong?* I had barely done anything. It made no sense.

Feeling a deep sense of shame, I didn't want to tell anyone. How could I explain how awful I felt after such a simple activity? I wanted to hide it and dismiss it.

It took a while before I felt enough strength return for me to be able to get up from the floor and sit back in my chair. But even sitting, I felt weak and sick, with all my energy sapped.

That evening, I reluctantly told my husband what had happened at work.

"That's not normal," Dumitru immediately told me. "You need to see a doctor."

"Okay," I finally agreed. "I'll call tomorrow."

3

Preliminary Diagnosis

After telling all my symptoms to Dr. Moore, my long-time internal medicine physician, he examined me, listening to my lungs and my heart.

"When did these symptoms first start?" he asked me.

"Well, actually, I've noticed this on and off for about two years," I told him. "But it was very mild before, and it has suddenly gotten worse lately."

"I don't find anything wrong," he said. "Everything seems fine."

"But something is not right," I insisted.

Dr. Moore thought for a minute. "Let's draw some blood, get a chest x-ray, run an EKG, and do some pulmonary function tests," he finally said, writing up the orders.

Desperate to get answers, I went directly to the lab next door and got my blood drawn. Then I drove up the street to the out-patient radiology center and handed them the prescription for my chest x-ray. After waiting about 40 minutes, they took several x-rays of my chest. Hoping that I would soon know what was wrong, I then got dressed and drove home.

The next day I went to the hospital, next door to my doctor's office, and went to the cardiology department. I undressed from the waist up, put on a hospital gown, and lay down on a table for the EKG. They hooked up all the sticky tapes and wires and ran the test, which was completely painless. When that was completed, they unhooked me, and I got dressed.

From there I went to the respiratory department for the pulmonary function tests. I sat in a small chamber, and multiple times I took deep breaths, blew into a machine, held my breath, blew some more, and then repeated it all again. I performed various other breathing tests with the machine, all of which were extremely uncomfortable. I did all these tests first without using an inhaler, and then again after using an inhaler, and all that testing took a long time.

When the testing was finally over, they told me that my lungs were functioning at only about 60% capacity, and that there was also inflammation in the area. I wasn't sure what to make of that.

About a week later, I returned to Dr. Moore's office to discuss the test results.

"Lynn, the chest x-rays show that your heart is somewhat enlarged," he told me, "but that is not necessarily a problem."

"My heart is enlarged?"

"Yes, but I wouldn't worry about that at this point. And based on the pulmonary function tests, your condition is possibly a form of asthma."

"Asthma?"

"Yes. I'm going to give you an inhaler to see if that will help."

He gave me an inhaler and showed me how to use it. Then he wrote a prescription for more in case I needed it.

"Let's see if this will help. If the problem continues or gets worse, then come back," he said, closing the file folder that he was holding and signaling the end of the visit.

A couple weeks later, on a warm Saturday afternoon at the end of April, we went to a birthday party for five-year-old twins of our good friends, who were also in the Sierra Club. We had been looking forward to this party and sharing in the celebration.

Carrying our brightly-colored wrapped gifts, with the ribbons flapping in the warm breeze, we joyfully arrived at the small children's gym, which they had rented for the party.

Festive music filled the room, and a group of children played happily on nearby mats. We joyfully greeted our friends and talked with them, getting caught up with the latest news.

After watching the children play and jump around on the foam mats, one of our friends picked up a 12-inch rubber ball. *Fun!* Playful and laughing, a few of us threw the ball back and forth to each other.

Suddenly, I could not breathe. Weak, dizzy, light-headed, and overwhelmed with a sickening feeling, I backed out of the circle. Completely depleted of energy and feeling like I was about to pass out, I quickly lay down on the nearest mat. I didn't care where I was or who saw me.

Dumitru immediately kneeled down next to me. "Are you okay?" he asked, gently rubbing my back.

I could not answer.

A minute later, I felt Dumitru shaking me. "Lynn!" he called out, his voice sounding like it was from a great distance away.

I groaned.

"What happened?" I heard someone ask.

"She passed out," my husband answered them.

"Lynn?" My husband stroked my hair.

"I just need to rest," I mumbled, barely audible.

My husband sat with me for about 30 minutes, while I lay there, dizzy and weak, covered in sweat, until I had the strength to sit up.

"You need to go back to the doctor," he insisted.

I nodded, feeling weak and dazed.

After we got home, we discussed what had happened. It was now the end of April, and we were looking forward to going to Maui in two weeks, the second week in May, to celebrate our ten-year anniversary.

"Let me use the inhaler for a couple more weeks and see if that helps. We can wait until after our vacation," I told my husband. "If I don't feel better by the time we are back from Maui, I will go back to the doctor then."

4

Going to Maui

Eagerly anticipating our vacation in Hawaii, we agreed to let go of our medical concerns for now, and we prepared for our trip. I figured that we could enjoy our anniversary on the beaches of Maui, and then deal with any medical issues when we returned. A few weeks shouldn't make a difference.

I researched online about what there was to see and do in Maui. Intrigued by the tours I saw and the bargain rates I was finding, I booked a few of the tours.

As my husband loved kayaking, I booked one tour where we would kayak out into the ocean, jump into the water and go snorkeling among the fish and giant sea turtles, and then kayak back to shore. The tour sounded really exciting, and we were especially looking forward to that one.

After checking our luggage at LAX airport in Los Angeles, we took our time and slowly walked to our gate, stopping often to rest. We had allowed plenty of time, so we were not rushed, and we had no problems. Our flight was on time, and we giggled like little kids as our plane flew us to Maui on that Sunday morning.

Getting off the plane in Maui, we were immediately enveloped by the tropical heat and humidity. We were greeted with fragrant leis, and wearing them helped us relax and get into the laid-back aloha mood of Hawaii. The airport was small, so there was minimal walking, and it didn't take long for us to get our luggage.

We picked up our rental car, drove to our hotel, and checked into our ocean-view room. The view was incredible – we could see palm trees, the pool, the beach, and the deep blue ocean. We were ecstatic.

We ran out to explore and see what else was there. The hotel grounds, meandering pools, palm trees, and the beach were magnificent and inviting. Simply being there and smelling the fragrant flowers along with the warm, salty, moist air, was amazing.

Feeling hungry, we took seats at a table on the terrace overlooking the ocean. We enjoyed a late lunch of seared Ahi, and we excitedly discussed our plans and tours for the next five days.

The next day, Monday, I slept in while Dumitru got up at 2:00 A.M. to go on a bicycle trip down Haleakala, a local dormant volcano. While he was away on his bike trip, I leisurely strolled around the hotel grounds, relaxing and enjoying the atmosphere.

When my husband got back from his trip, we shared a delicious lunch of Mahi Mahi on the hotel grounds, overlooking the beach, while he excitedly told me all about the bike tour.

After lunch we drove up the main road to explore the coast north of our hotel and search for a blowhole that was listed in my tour book.

We parked our rental car where we saw the indicated marker, and then we got out to explore. Since Dumitru and I were avid hikers, it was natural for us to hike and explore on rough terrain. However, after my recent medical problems, I decided not to push myself.

When we saw that the blowhole was down at the bottom of a steep trail, I chose to stay at the top, while Dumitru ran down to the blowhole and check it out.

"You didn't miss much," Dumitru told me after he climbed back up. "The blowhole was small, so it was good that you stayed at the top and didn't strain yourself."

We walked around the area a little more, but I quickly found that I did not have the strength or stamina to walk very far.

"I'm not up to walking around or exploring more," I told Dumitru. "I just feel too tired and weak."

My husband understood, and we returned to the hotel. The rest of the afternoon we sat on the beach behind our hotel, and we gently waded into the ocean.

Tuesday morning we went on an ATV tour of the upcountry. As this tour was almost all sitting and there was minimal walking, I had no problems, and we enjoyed the spectacular scenery and the picnic lunch.

In the afternoon, we went to Lahaina and walked around, checking out the famous Banyan tree and going into the local gift shops. Tiring quickly, I simply wanted to leave, so we did not stay long. I couldn't wait to get back to our hotel and just rest.

I also wanted to make sure that I was well rested and had energy for our kayak tour, which was the next day.

5

Kayak Tour

On Wednesday, we were booked on the much-anticipated kayak-and-snorkel tour. It was going to be an incredible thrill, and we couldn't wait!

The morning was warm and sunny, and we drove down the main road, looking for a specific marker at the side of the road, which was where we would be meeting for the kayak excursion. A few miles farther down the road, admiring the scenery and seeing the sun glinting off the ocean, we finally saw the marker. We pulled off the road and parked under some trees.

Some kayaks were on the side, with a few people standing near them. One of the people, Kevin, was the guide for the tour, and we approached him and quickly introduced ourselves.

Once everyone was checked in and had signed the release papers, Kevin went over the rules of what to do, what not to do, how to paddle, and how to stay safe. I barely paid attention, as my husband and I had kayaked together many times, and we were excited and anxious to get going.

After everyone on the tour grabbed a life vest, flippers, and snorkeling gear, we were ready to go. The day was warm and mild; there were a few clouds out over the horizon, but the sky above was bright blue and clear.

My husband and I got into the two-person kayak, and we pushed off into the clear turquoise water. Dumitru leaned forward from the back seat. "Don't forget," he told me. "I will do most of the work, and you can rest. Only paddle a little bit if you're up to it."

"Okay," I answered, the paddle resting on my lap, as I happily gazed at the sunlight sparkling on the surface of the water. Dumitru was proficient at competitive kayaking, so I was comfortable with letting him do almost all the work.

Including us, there were three kayaks plus Kevin, and we all paddled out into the ocean, our group staying close to our guide in front of us. As we moved through the gentle water, everyone was pointing at the spectacular fish and giant sea turtles that we saw along the way.

After about 30 minutes of kayaking, during which I had only paddled occasionally, the guide stopped paddling and came to a stop. Our group quickly gathered around his boat.

"Okay," Kevin instructed, "this is where we can jump into the water and go snorkeling. Let's tie our kayaks together so we don't lose anyone, and then feel free to jump into the water when you're ready."

Everyone murmured agreement as the guide helped tie the boats together.

I was happy, and I couldn't wait to jump into the 80-degree water.

"Do we need to wear our life vests?" I asked Kevin.

"Only if you want to, it's up to you," he answered.

I joked to Kevin that since I had a high fat content in my body, I could practically walk on the water.

"I'd like to see that," he replied, laughing.

I giggled with delight and looked out over the crystal-clear water.

Most of the kayakers put their life vests on, but my husband and I decided not to wear ours. We both were excellent swimmers and saw no need for them.

Leaving the life vests in the kayak, my husband and I quickly dove into the warm, tropical water. It felt so silky smooth and was such a thrill. Coming up to the surface, I laughed out loud with delight.

The water felt heavenly, and I eagerly started swimming through the warm, gentle waves. After only a few strokes, I suddenly knew something was horribly wrong.

I was quickly overcome with an awful feeling of overwhelming weakness and a profound, debilitating lack of energy. I was dizzy, light-headed, and could barely breathe. My body felt almost paralyzed. My energy was depleted, and I felt strange and constricted. I somehow had no air and could not move.

Unable to even tread water, I could not stay afloat, and I could not raise my voice to call out for help. My husband took one look at my face and knew I was in trouble. "What's wrong?" he asked, concern all over his face.

"I can't move," I barely whispered, "I can't breathe. Can I lean on you?"

"Yes," he said, and I reached toward him, placing my hands on his shoulders.

He started sinking and looked scared, as he struggled to keep both of us afloat.

"No," he pleaded, panic in his voice. "You're pushing me under. I can't keep us both up. Ask the guide."

Seeing that there was a problem, Kevin swam over to us. "Can I lean on you?" I whispered.

"Yes, of course," Kevin answered.

I gratefully clung to him, dead weight, and barely breathing.

"I'll go get your life vest," Dumitru said, and he swam as fast as he could back to the kayak to retrieve my life vest.

Years of meditating kicked in, and I kept telling myself to just relax and stay calm. Feeling sickeningly constricted, I repeated the words over and over. *Relax and stay calm.*

Somehow I knew that if I panicked, I could easily pass out and the situation could become much worse. Hardly able to get a breath, I clung to Kevin, hoping to survive, until my husband returned with the life vest.

Dumitru swam back with the life vest, his eyes filled with fear. I clutched the life vest, and the guide pulled me back to the kayak, while my husband swam at my side.

Once back at the boat, I didn't know what to do. How could I possibly get into it? With absolutely no energy and my body almost lifeless, I was too weak; there was no way I could climb in.

"Don't worry," Kevin said to me, "I'll get you into the kayak. But first, just hold onto the side and wait until your strength starts coming back."

I nodded, barely breathing. It took maybe 10 or 15 minutes of just holding onto the side of the kayak before I started feeling better. Kevin then gave me instructions on what to do.

"Don't fight it, just let me pull you in," he told me. *I'm too fat and heavy,* I thought, *this is impossible.* But I relaxed and positioned my body the way he instructed, and before I knew it, he had effortlessly pulled me into the kayak.

I had no idea how he did it, but I was extremely relieved and grateful to now be sitting up in the kayak. Wheezing, I then coughed up some mucus.

"I'm so sorry," I said to the guide.

"Are you okay?" he asked, concern in his voice.

"I think I have asthma," I said. "Thank you for helping me."

Embarrassed by the entire episode, I didn't want to say more. I did not think that this really was asthma, but I had no idea what was actually wrong.

Kevin then stayed in the kayak with me and made sure I was okay and did not need additional help.

On the return trip back to shore, I sat barely moving, while Dumitru did all the paddling. Dazed and confused, all I wanted to do was get back to the hotel.

After reaching the shore and getting out of the kayak, we thanked Kevin, assured him that I was okay, and we gave him a big tip.

"You're going back to the doctor as soon as we get home," Dumitru told me as he drove us back to our hotel.

Doing almost nothing the rest of the day, we stayed on the hotel grounds, sat on the beach, and watched the ocean waves gently lapping onto the golden sand.

We still had two more full days to get through before we flew home, and I prayed that I would not die on Maui that week.

6

Difficulty Walking

Thursday morning, we were booked on a snorkel tour at Molokini, which is a volcanic crater just off the Maui coast, with a protected area known for spectacular snorkeling. We drove the short distance to the harbor, and then we boarded the boat. Draped in fear and trepidation, we sat huddled together on a bench on the lower level.

"Stay with me," I implored.

"I'm not letting you out of my sight," he replied.

When we reached Molokini and it was time to get in the water, I took two flotation devices. I wore a life vest, and I also grabbed and held onto a foam paddle board. I desperately wanted to make sure that I had support if needed, and that I would use minimal effort and not exert myself.

One of the young crew members watched me put on the flippers, and then he helped me get down to the last step off the back of the boat, hovering above the water.

"I used to be a good swimmer," I told him, tightly clutching the flotation board.

"Oh, back in the day?" he said and laughed.

Back in the day? I wondered how old he thought I was, but I just smiled and eased into the water.

Between the life vest and the foam board, it was effortless to stay afloat, and I slowly and easily glided along the surface of the water, looking down at the fish below me. The fish were amazing to see – so many of them in brilliant colors. Dumitru stayed right next to me the whole time.

I was so glad when it was over, and we were back on the boat without incident. Without saying another word to each other, we ate a barbecue lunch on board, as the boat headed back to shore.

That afternoon, we sat on the beach and just rested. I couldn't wait to go home, and I knew that I had to hang on for one more day. I hoped that the next day would be easy.

The following day, Friday, we needed to visit one last place – the botanical gardens. We drove there, hoping that there would be no problem. The gardens were absolutely beautiful – spectacular, in fact.

It felt a little too warm and humid for hiking, and I was a little uncomfortable. However, we were only going to be there that one time, and I wanted to see all the unusual and striking tropical plants and flora.

Concrete paths meandered invitingly throughout the gardens. When they gently angled downhill, they were easy to navigate. But when they angled uphill, even slightly, I could not walk at all.

"Push," I said, as I slowed down almost to a stop. My husband got behind me and pushed, and I was then able to slowly make my way up the gradual inclines.

After about 20 minutes, I found that I could no longer walk even on level ground. My strength, energy, stamina, and oxygen were depleted. I felt like an empty shell, barely alive, completely drained of energy. We were on flat, level ground, and I suddenly could not move. I barely had the energy to softly whisper one word. "Push," was all I could say.

And my wonderful husband, with the patience of a saint, pushed me forward along the level concrete path.

Dumitru kept looking at me and checking on me. I could tell from the concern in his eyes that I must have looked awful.

∽~∾

Saturday finally arrived, and thankfully we were flying home that day.

We drove to the airport, returned the rental car, and slowly trudged to our gate. Fortunately, with such a small airport, it was not a long walk.

At the gate, we saw that our plane was sitting out on the tarmac a short distance away, and that we would need to walk out to it and climb stairs in order to board. *Would I be able to make it up the stairs?*

We then heard an announcement requesting that anyone who needed assistance or who needed to pre-board should come forward and speak to an agent. Dumitru and I looked at each other, and I nodded.

He approached the gate and spoke to the lady behind the desk. She immediately smiled and handed my husband a pre-boarding pass, and I felt relief flooding through me.

When they later called for boarding for passengers who were pre-boarding or who needed assistance, we got up and slowly walked outside toward the plane. At first I felt a little silly and wondered if this was really necessary, but I quickly found that the stairs took most of my strength.

I needed to stop, rest, and catch my breath after every three or four steps upward. It took more than five minutes to reach the top of the stairs and enter the plane, but we finally made it. After we settled into our seats, I gratefully relaxed, as the mass of passengers then hustled in and noisily tromped down the aisle.

Holding tightly onto my husband's hand through most of the flight home, I prayed that I would stay alive at least until I could get to my doctor.

After landing at LAX airport in Los Angeles, I told my husband that I needed a wheelchair. "I can't walk this huge airport," I told him. I suddenly realized that I felt weaker and much worse now than when we had first come to the airport just six days earlier.

Dumitru spoke to someone at the nearest service desk to request a wheelchair. Within a few minutes, an electric shuttle, with bench seats, wheeled up next to us. "Did you need a lift?" the driver asked us, smiling.

"Yes, please," Dumitru answered, as we stood up and approached the shuttle. "We need to go to baggage claim," he told the driver.

The driver helped me climb on, and then the shuttle silently and swiftly made its way through miles of corridors to the baggage claim. After seeing the huge distance that we traveled, I knew without any doubt that I could not have walked that distance on my own.

7

THE ECHOCARDIOGRAM

Throughout that first week back home at the end of May, it became clear that I was definitely getting worse. My condition was noticeably deteriorating. I could now barely walk 20 feet without getting winded and needing to sit and catch my breath.

However, I delayed calling the doctor for another week. I called Dr. Moore the first week in June and made an appointment for the following week.

Over the next few days, I realized that I was left breathless, weak, and devoid of energy even after simply going down our short driveway to pick up the newspaper and bring it back to the house. Whatever was wrong, it was getting profoundly and disturbingly worse.

On Monday, June 13, I went to my appointment with Dr. Moore. In the doctor's office, I explained what had happened, how bad it was, and that it was continuing to get worse.

This time Dr. Moore ordered an echocardiogram to check the functioning of my heart.

I immediately went next door to the hospital cardiology department, and I showed them the prescription for an echocardiogram. I was told to undress from the waist up and to put on a dressing gown.

Although I was worried about what would be entailed, the test was not painful. However, it took longer than I expected. Similar to an ultrasound examination, gel was put on a contact which was then moved over different areas of my chest, while a technician viewed a screen and recorded the images showing the functioning of my heart.

The technician kept pressing the contact over the same area many times, as he intently watched the screen. I asked the technician if he saw anything wrong, but all he kept saying was, "The doctor will speak to you." After getting dressed, I went home.

By the time I reached the house, maybe 20 minutes later, there was already a message waiting for me on my answering machine. It was Dr. Moore asking me to call him immediately.

I called his office, and he quickly got on the phone. There was an intensity in his voice. "I need you to come back to the office today," he said. "Can you come right now?"

Glancing at the clock I saw that it was already 4:30 in the afternoon. I said okay, and I drove back to his office. He looked at me, and I realized that I had never seen him so serious. This was a doctor who I had known for over ten years, and we had developed a comfortable relationship and friendly banter with each other. But now he was not smiling like he usually did, and his face was grim.

He did not bother with any pleasantries. "There is a problem with one of your heart valves," he said. "This is serious. You need surgery immediately. I have a cardiologist standing by, waiting to talk to you. He is the top cardiologist in the area."

"What?" I said dumbly, barely understanding him.

"Lynn, you have severe aortic stenosis," he explained. "Your aortic valve is not functioning properly. It is rigid and is no longer opening and closing the way it should. It is stuck in a closed position, less than 0.6 centimeters."

He paused, cleared his throat, and then continued. "This is fatal. The valve must be replaced. The cardiologist said this needs immediate surgery, and you have to call him and see him right away. He's waiting for you to call." He then handed me a card with a cardiologist's name on it.

I looked at Dr. Moore, waiting for a smile and a punch line, but none came. Meekly, I muttered, "Really?"

"Yes, and you will need open-heart surgery." I simply stared at him in response. "Do you understand?" the doctor asked me. He looked intently at me, and I nodded.

I asked him one more question. "What would happen if I don't have this surgery?"

Dr. Moore looked back at me, hesitated, and then clearly said, "You will die."

I was silent for a minute. "Can I use a bad word?"

He smiled. "Yes."

"Fuck, fuck, fuck, fuck, fuck," I said.

I left his office, gripping the cardiologist's business card. I felt confused and overwhelmed. *A defective heart valve? Aortic stenosis? Open-heart surgery? What?* I drove home in a daze.

Since it was already after business hours, I would have to call the cardiologist the next day. So in the meantime, I went online and looked up information about aortic stenosis. What I found terrified and sickened me.

I read that most patients die within one or two years from the onset of symptoms. I had had symptoms for at least two years. It said that normally the aortic valve opened to 3 centimeters. Severe stenosis was 0.8 cm. My doctor had told me that mine was less than 0.6 cm.

Now I understood what was happening and why I had been feeling the way I had. My aortic valve was rigid and stuck in a closed position, which meant that oxygenated blood was not effectively getting to the rest of my body. That was why I was running out of air, was out of energy, and why I was passing out. And I realized that I definitely could die from this – at any time.

The next day, early in the morning on Tuesday, June 14, I called the cardiologist's office. They were waiting for my call, and they told me to come in right away. Scared and confused, I drove to his office.

The cardiologist looked to be in his late 50s, and he had a round, kind face, topped with a mop of white hair. "Hi Lynn, I'm Dr. Tillman," he said, greeting me warmly. "How are you feeling?"

"I feel weak, out of breath a lot, and scared," I answered him.

He asked me to get up on the table, and I did. Dr. Tillman observed how I was panting and out of breath from the effort to do that small task. He looked at me for a moment, evaluating what he saw.

"Have you been passing out?" he asked.

"Yes," I answered quietly.

He stopped smiling, looked at me intently, and he said, "This is serious. The next time you pass out, you might not wake up." He waited a few beats to make sure that sunk in.

Then he continued. "You do not have asthma. You have severe aortic stenosis, which means that your aortic valve is rigid and almost closed. All your symptoms are from the faulty aortic valve."

He glanced at his notes and then continued. "Most people's aortic valves have three cusps, but yours has only two – it is a bicuspid valve, and aortic stenosis is more common with bicuspid valves. Right now," he explained, "your aortic valve is open less than 0.6 cm, and that is critical." He wrote something in a chart and then looked up at me. "I want you to have the surgery done right away, within two days."

"That soon?" I asked.

"Absolutely. You are already in congestive heart failure, and your condition is getting worse. You need surgery immediately. I want you to go into the hospital tomorrow, Wednesday, to have an angiogram. I want to make sure that there are no other surprises, such as blocked arteries which would need a bypass." He paused and then continued, "And then I want to have the surgery done on Thursday."

"Can I have just one more day? I need to inform my employer and take care of a few things. Can I go to the hospital on Thursday for the angiogram and have the surgery on Friday? Is that okay?"

Dr. Tillman hesitated, and then said, "Okay."

Tapping the medical file on the table, he then said, "You will have to decide whether you want a mechanical valve or a tissue valve. A mechanical valve would be permanent and last the rest of your life, but you would always hear a metallic clicking sound inside you. And," he added, "you would need to be on Coumadin, a blood thinner, for the rest of your life. On the other hand," he explained, "a tissue valve would last maybe 10 to 15 years, and it would come from a pig or a cow. You would not need to be on any blood thinners at all, but you would need another open-heart surgery in 10 or 15 years to replace the valve again."

"I will need to think about it," I said.

"You have just a couple days to decide," he said. "We'll put in whichever valve you prefer."

I left his office in a fog, not sure of what was happening or which valve to choose. Everything was happening too fast, and I didn't know what to do.

8

Going Downhill

My parents were out of the country on vacation at that time, and that disturbed me – they did not know anything about this. *What if they were to come back from vacation to find out that their daughter had not only had emergency open-heart surgery, but had died, while they were on vacation?*

That horrified me, and I didn't want to even think about that. *No, no, no – think happy thoughts.* Trying to distract myself, I got on the computer.

I researched online about mechanical valves and tissue valves, about Coumadin, and about open-heart surgery. The huge amount of information that I found was overwhelming, and I still did not know which type of valve to choose, but I knew that I did not have much time to decide.

And now I was scared to go to sleep. If severe stenosis was 0.8 cm, and I was under 0.6 cm, that was really critical. I could die at any time, any moment. I felt like I was on borrowed time. *What if I didn't wake up the next morning? What if I died in my sleep that night?* I stayed awake for a while, holding my husband's hand. *Would I wake up tomorrow?*

When I woke up the next morning, I felt surprised, relieved, and thankful. *I was still alive!* I called my boss at work and let her know that I was going into the hospital for emergency open-heart surgery and would not be back for a couple months.

It became very clear that even on a daily basis, I was definitely getting worse. I had severe shortness of breath with even less exertion than before. Just getting up from a chair or walking across a room, or simply walking from one room to the next, got me winded and huffing and puffing. I could barely talk on the phone, as I no longer had the strength to project my voice.

My husband was now helping me get dressed because I got too winded bending down. He was with me every second and was not letting me out of his sight. Although he tried not to show it, I knew he was scared.

I questioned a few people about the different heart valve options, and I did more research online, trying to decide which valve would be the better choice.

Since I was the one who paid the bills in our house, I reviewed all the bills with my husband, and I taught him my system for paying them. I showed him what was paid and what was not yet paid, and how to pay the bills online, in case I did not survive the surgery.

As my parents were still out of the country for a few more days, I could not reach them. I e-mailed everyone else I knew – family, friends, and an online spiritual network in which I was involved – that I was going in for open-heart surgery, and that instead of feeling sorry for me, they all should picture me happy and healthy.

That helped me feel somewhat prepared, as I now had in place a supportive network of people who would send me healing energy, light, thoughts, prayers, and positive images over the next few days to help me through the surgery and with my recovery.

That night I was again scared to go to sleep. I told my husband I loved him, and I prayed that I would wake up the next day.

On Thursday, June 16, a cool and cloudy morning, my husband drove me to the hospital – Providence Holy Cross Medical Center, in Mission Hills, California. On the 20-minute drive to the hospital, I held tightly to the armrest and watched the billowy gray clouds floating slowly across the sky.

After parking the car, Dumitru held my hand, and we walked across the parking lot and into the hospital. Shakily, I entered the admissions department, told them why I was there, and I filled out all their forms.

In a wheelchair, I was then taken to a small, dimly-lit waiting area to wait for the angiogram. I was scared. Various nurses came to talk to me and explain things about the procedure. It was a whirlwind of words, some of which I understood, and some of which I did not. In a shaky fog, I changed into a hospital gown.

Someone stuck a needle in the back of my right hand, which was very painful, and they hooked up an IV. Cold, scared, and shivering, I was then placed on a gurney. Noticing that my teeth were chattering, a nurse brought me a blanket.

I wanted to calm down. I tried to think of anything calming, but that did not help. Then I remembered the network of people sending me good thoughts, prayers, and healing energy. Imagining the warm, loving, healing energy flowing into me helped for a few seconds, and then I started shivering with fear again.

Someone wheeled me into another room, swabbed at my groin area, and stuck a needle into my femoral artery. I did not feel anything. The doctor looked at an image on a screen and said that there were no blockages, my arteries were fine, and everything looked good. However, the doctor told me that my aortic valve was now closed down to 0.4 cm.

They took out whatever had been inserted in my femoral artery, and an intense heat filled my entire groin area. The doctor then pressed down very hard on the femoral artery. After a few minutes, an assistant switched with him.

"Is he pressing down as hard as I was?" the doctor asked me.

"Yes."

"Good, because I don't want you to bleed out. If he lets up on the pressure, tell me immediately."

The doctor then told me that I could not move that leg at all for at least four hours, and that I could not even sit up to eat, for fear of the puncture site in the femoral artery bleeding again.

After the angiogram was over, they told me that they needed to roll me over and transfer me to another gurney, and they were adamant that I not move. They warned me that it will feel like I am falling, but that I needed to trust them. They assured me that they had me, and not to shift at all.

They were right – it felt like I was falling, but I didn't move, and they supported me and transferred me to the gurney. Then I was wheeled to an elevator and brought upstairs to a private room. I lay there immobile, afraid to budge, for more than four hours.

Dumitru made sure I was settled down and relaxed, and then he went home, promising to be back first thing the next morning.

I was hooked up to various monitors and IVs. There were wires and hoses coming out of my body, and I found it annoying. Any time I needed to go to the bathroom, I had to drag all the cords, monitors, IVs, and various things with me. But I knew that now, if anything went wrong, at least I was in a hospital, I was being monitored, and I was surrounded by medical professionals. I would be okay.

A handsome man with dark hair came to see me. "Hi," he began, "I'm Dr. Soldano. I'm the cardiac surgeon, and I will be doing the valve replacement surgery on you tomorrow." He seemed strong and confident, and I liked him right away. "Do you have any questions?" he asked me.

"How many of these surgeries have you done?"

"In my career, thousands," he answered. I liked that.

"What kind of valve do you want?" he asked. When I hesitated, he continued. "We usually recommend that people in their 30s get the mechanical valve, and that people in their 70s get the tissue valve," he explained. "However, you are in the middle, in your early 50s, and it's up to you."

"I'm not sure."

"The tissue valves now last longer than they used to," he added. "We are finding that they now are lasting maybe 15-20 years."

"Maybe a mechanical valve so I won't have to do this again," I told him.

"Okay," he replied. "That's fine; I will put in a mechanical valve."

"Which would you choose if it was you having this surgery?"

"I would get a tissue valve," he answered without hesitation.

"How old are you?" I asked, wondering if he was around my age, in case age figured into the decision.

"I'm 58," he said.

He was just a little older than me, and since that is what he would have chosen, I now wondered if I should get the tissue valve instead.

Then he left, and I was still debating which to choose.

As every nurse came into my room that day, I asked each one of them which valve they would choose.

"I would *never* want to be on Coumadin," one nurse told me. "There are too many potential problems and complications."

"Blood thinners like Coumadin often cause a lot of problems," another nurse said. "We see it all the time. There's no way I would want to be on Coumadin if I had a choice."

"Coumadin levels need to be constantly monitored," another nurse told me, "so you would need to keep going to the doctor every month and get your blood drawn. I would not want to be on Coumadin."

After talking to each nurse who came into my room, I realized that it was unanimous – every one of them said that they would choose the tissue valve and that they would not want to be on Coumadin.

After evaluating what the nurses had told me, I changed my mind and decided that I now wanted a tissue valve. *Was it too late?*

I asked a nurse to tell the cardiac surgeon that I had changed my mind and that I wanted a tissue valve. She said okay, she would let him know. As the surgery was scheduled for the following morning, I hoped that he would get the message in time.

A short time later, the anesthesiologist came and talked to me. He was soft-spoken and kind, and he did not stay very long.

A nurse told me that I could have dinner, but that I could not have anything after midnight, not even water. To be extra safe, I decided to have nothing after 10:00 P.M.

One of the nurses gave me a booklet to read about what to expect during open-heart surgery. It covered what they do, what happens, what to expect during my hospital stay, and what would happen in recovery. The details in the description turned my stomach and made me queasy. I opened the booklet a few times, but I could not focus on or absorb any of the information as it was too overwhelming, and I put the booklet aside.

After dinner, I was left alone for a while with nothing but my thoughts and my fears, which soon got the better of me. *What if I did not survive the surgery? What if I was meant to die? What if I had made such a mess of things here on earth that I did not deserve to live? What if God decided I had wasted my life and that it was time for me to die? What if I was simply not good enough and simply did not deserve to continue living?*

Would my doubts hurt my chances of surviving? Would I survive open-heart surgery if my will to live was not strong enough? Would I die tomorrow? Was this my last night on earth?

In the evening, a nurse came in and told me to take a shower and to wash my chest with a special soap. I did as she requested, and then I crawled back into bed. I tried to watch TV but was unable to focus, and I turned it off.

I called home and spoke with my husband. He said he would be there first thing in the morning and stay with me all day.

Then I simply lay in bed, listening to the various noises drifting in from the other rooms on the hospital floor, and I tried to stay relaxed and calm.

Tossing and turning, I slept restlessly throughout the night.

9

Open-Heart Surgery

In the early morning on Friday, June 17, the nurse came to my room to give me a pill. Surprised, I told her that I'm not supposed to have anything by mouth. She said that the doctor ordered it, and it was for inflammation. Thinking she must be mistaken, I told her no, and she threw out the pill.

Worried about it, I then called my husband and told him what had just happened. He said that if the doctor had ordered it, I should take the pill. So I then called the nurse back and told her yes, I'll take it. But since she had already thrown out the pill, she needed to order a new one from the pharmacy.

That made me anxious – *would I get it in time? Did it make a difference if I took it late?* It took over an hour to get the replacement pill sent up, and I was relieved when she finally brought it to me. Hoping it was okay to take it and that I wasn't screwing up anything, I then took the pill with a tiny sip of water.

Dr. Soldano, the cardiac surgeon, stopped by. I told him that I had changed my mind and now wanted the tissue valve, and I asked him if he had gotten the message, and if that was okay.

"Yes, I got the message. And it's no problem, I will put in a tissue valve." He took a step closer. "How are you feeling?"

"I have a slight sore throat," I said quietly.

"Do you want to postpone the surgery?"

"No, no, I think I just didn't sleep well, don't postpone it." I was suddenly worried that I might not live long enough if I had to wait for another time.

"Okay, we'll do it today."

"Please do a good job," I whispered.

He smiled at me. "That's my goal, too."

Then I was left alone for a while. Two hours passed. *Did someone not remember to come get me? Was there a problem? Was the surgery still scheduled for that morning?*

A little while later, someone came into the room and had me climb onto a gurney and lie down. He then wheeled me out of the room, down the hallway, and into an elevator.

The elevator went down, and my stomach flipped – lying flat in a moving elevator was a totally different feeling than when you're standing up, and I didn't expect it.

Then I was wheeled down another hallway into a waiting area in the surgical suite, and I was left there for a while. Nervous and worried, I kept clenching my fists, and it seemed like a long time passed. *Did anyone know I was there? Did they forget about me? Had I been left in the wrong place?* I started shaking again with fear.

After more time passed, someone came and wheeled me into another room. Someone with a mask on his face leaned over and asked if I was okay, and if I had any questions.

"When will I get the valium IV?" I asked.

I heard him chuckle and saw him smile behind his mask. "In just a few minutes," he answered. I felt his hand rest on my arm, and I calmed down a little bit.

A few minutes later, someone started the valium in the IV, and within seconds, I drifted into a deep sleep.

While I slept, a breathing tube was placed down my throat and into my lungs, and the tube was connected to a ventilator, which breathed for me. A catheter was inserted.

Dr. Soldano made a six-inch incision down the center of my chest. Then my breastbone was cut, and my rib cage was spread and clamped open.

A heart-lung bypass machine was connected to my heart, and my heart was stopped. A tube was placed in my heart to drain blood to the machine. This machine removed carbon dioxide, added oxygen, and then pumped the blood back into my body, thereby taking over the pumping action of my heart. The blood was also drastically cooled through the heart-lung machine to help lower my body temperature. A tube was inserted into my chest to drain the fluid.

The surgeon could now operate on my heart while it was not beating and without blood flowing through it. He carefully and painstakingly removed the defective aortic valve and replaced it with an artificial valve made of tissue from a cow. After the valve was replaced, blood flow was restored, and they re-started the beating of my heart.

Once my heart was beating, the surgeon removed the tubes and stopped the heart-lung bypass machine. My ribs were put back in place, and metal wires were used to close my breastbone and hold it together. Stitches were then used to close the incision on my chest.

I was then wheeled into ICU for monitoring, with an IV, a catheter, a tube in my throat, and tubes coming out of my chest to aid in drainage.

Still asleep for a while, I rested peacefully in the ICU, blissfully unaware of any of this.

10

RECOVERY IN THE ICU

The next thing I knew, I was hearing my husband's voice from a distance, almost as if in a dream. Then I realized that he was right next to me, on my left. I was hearing him talking to a nurse about how we met, and I felt my left hand being held in his hand.

I was elated – *I made it – I had survived! The surgery was over!* I was now awake in recovery somewhere, but I had no idea where. *And I was still alive! Yes!*

My husband was talking to a nurse, and he told her that he couldn't remember the name of the mountain where we had met and connected. I remembered – it was Mt. Baldy. Since both my husband and I knew sign language, I finger-spelled "B-A-L-D-Y" into his hand with my left hand.

My husband felt it – and he instantly realized what I was doing. He got really excited and started jabbering to the nurse about my signing "B-A-L-D-Y," and I felt happy and proud.

And then I was asleep again. I awoke some time later to a loud beeping and a nurse's voice yelling, "BREATHE!" *Huh?* I was now awake and breathing.

I heard the nurse explaining to my husband that they needed me to breathe on my own so that they could get me off the ventilator. The beeping was the alarm that I was not breathing on my own and that the ventilator had to breathe for me.

But I was so tired, and I kept falling asleep. And then I again woke up to a loud beeping and the nurse yelling, "BREATHE!" *But I'm tired, I want to sleep…*

After a while, I started breathing on my own, and the nurse said that they could now take out the breathing tube. Until she said that, I was not even aware that there was a tube down my throat.

My husband tried to warn the nurse that I choke easily, but she told him not to worry, that they are experienced with this. They counted down for me, and then the nurse asked me to exhale, which I did. And while I was exhaling, they easily slid the tube out with no problem. Then they put a little hose thing with prongs in my nose for oxygen, and I promptly went back to sleep.

I had needles, tubes, and wires coming out of my neck, my chest, and my arms, and these were hooked up to various kinds of equipment. All day and night in the ICU, there were continuous sounds of swishing, soft beeping, and gentle alarms, but they didn't bother me. I actually liked them and found them strangely soothing and comforting.

I was told that the surgery had gone well and that there were no complications. My husband stayed with me all day, as I slept on and off throughout the rest of the day, and in the evening he went home.

The following day, Saturday, June 18, the nurse woke me at 6:00 A.M., and she asked me to sit up and get out of bed. I thought she was nuts – *after open-heart surgery the day before, how was I supposed to move around?* She told me that my husband would be there between 6:30 and 7:00 that morning, and she wanted me sitting up in a chair and eating breakfast when he got there. She then brushed my teeth for me, which felt really good.

The nurse taught me that to sit up, first I had to raise the top half of the bed by pressing a button so that it would push me more upright. Then I had to turn and put my weight on my elbow, not my hands, in order to keep pressure off my chest. And I needed to hug a large, red, heart-shaped pillow with my arms, and stand up using only my legs, not my hands.

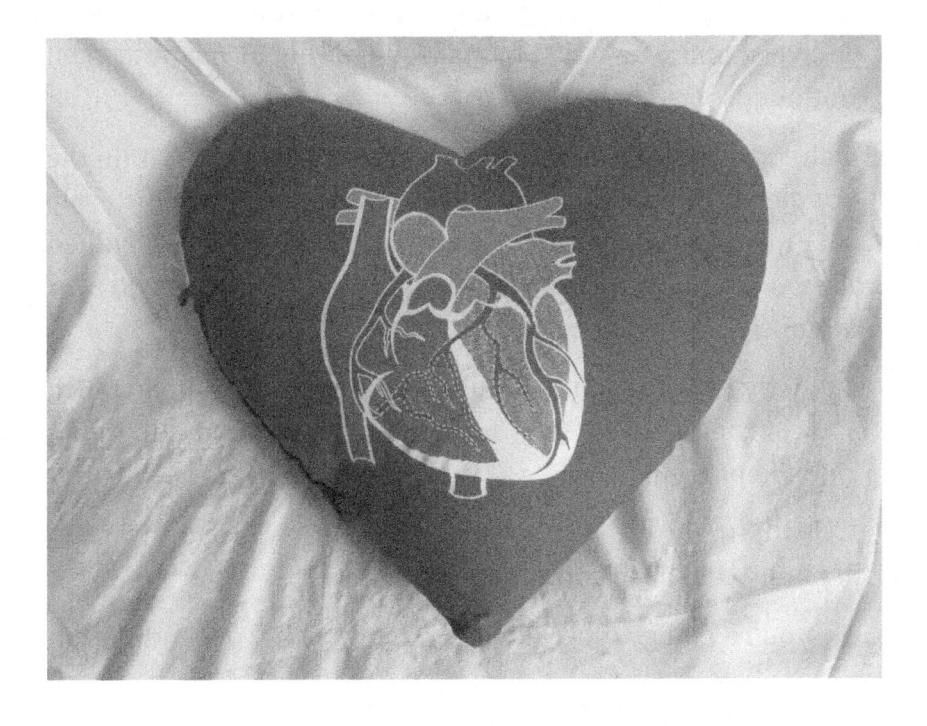

The nurse handed me the big red pillow and was very insistent about the procedures and the proper way to move. A bit shaky, I followed her instructions. I felt weak and wobbly but, holding onto the pillow, I was able to sit up, get out of bed, take a few steps, and sit down in a nearby chair.

The first day-time ICU nurse that I had was like an overbearing boot-camp instructor. She sternly lectured me for over 30 minutes on how I'd have to work hard and push myself and breathe and cough and walk. She harshly told me that she wouldn't let me get away with anything because it was so important to get moving, do everything she asked of me, and get the congestion out of my lungs.

"I won't let you take the easy way out and not do what you need to do," she yelled at me. "This is important, and you need to push yourself. This is for your own good, and you can't take it easy. I will hound you and constantly keep on you and make sure you do everything we ask." She paused, glaring at me. And then she continued, on and on.

I already knew all of that and had agreed with her within the first couple of minutes, but she didn't let up. She kept sternly lecturing me and yelling for so long that I started feeling bullied and abused, and I began crying. *I did not need a harsh lecture for 30 minutes the day after open-heart surgery.*

I quietly explained to her multiple times that I respond much better to encouragement than to being yelled at, but she didn't stop, and I kept crying.

"This is the way I am," she said abruptly. "Do you want to switch nurses and have another nurse instead?"

"If you're going to be like that, then yes, I want a different nurse."

She left the room, and another nurse came in who was much nicer. This new nurse apologized for the other nurse, and she said that that was her style. I explained to my new nurse that I respond better to encouragement than to being bullied, lectured, and criticized, and she seemed to understand. I felt somewhat relieved, but it took me a while to stop crying and to calm down.

My husband arrived after I had my new nurse. He came into the ICU room holding a stuffed doggie and a get-well Mylar balloon, and he stood there gazing at me, a shocked look on his face.

"Hi Honey, how are you feeling?" he asked, coming closer and putting the gifts on a nearby table.

"Okay."

"Wow – it's good to see you sitting up in a chair," he said, sounding surprised.

I smiled weakly.

He sat down in a chair next to me and rubbed my leg. "I expected you to be in bed all day."

"I can't do much," I said. It felt good to have him there.

He got up and briefly talked to the nurse, and then he came back, sat down again, and watched me eat a small bowl of oatmeal.

After breakfast, I clutched the big, red heart pillow and held it to my chest. I was supposed to cough to get the fluid out of my lungs, but coughing was extremely painful. I was told to hug that big pillow and press it into my sternum when I coughed to help relieve the pain.

The nurse came in and gave me a breathing apparatus called an incentive spirometer to help me cough. As instructed, I put my mouth over the mouthpiece, breathed in as deeply as I could, raising a piston as high as possible, held it a few seconds, and then exhaled. That made me cough, and I then desperately held the pillow against my breastbone. The pain was excruciating. The nurse explained that coughing was important because it helped remove any extra mucus or fluid in my lungs to help prevent pneumonia.

I needed to use this device every hour to help clear my lungs. I hated it and dreaded using it, but I did it. Over the next few hours, it became clear that I was raising the piston higher each time that I used it, so I knew that my lungs were getting stronger. I was glad for that, but coughing was still so horribly, excruciatingly painful.

It felt good to rest, and Dumitru sat with me all day. I slept in bed for a while, got up and sat in the chair a few times, took a few steps, and then went back to bed. Most of the day was spent resting, dozing, and listening to the beeps of the machines.

Any time I felt like I needed to shift position or roll over onto my side, I pushed a button and rang for the nurse. The nurses came to me almost instantly, making sure there was no emergency, and ready to help in whatever way I needed.

I felt a little guilty bothering them just for me to roll over, but I had no choice, as I could not do that myself. Holding my body straight and hugging the heart pillow, two nurses would pull me slightly to one edge of the bed and then carefully roll me onto my side. *Ahhh, that felt so much better.* Until I needed to shift again.

The nurses wanted me to eat as much as possible at meals and also in between meals to help me get my strength back. The food was actually delicious, but I ate very little.

Eating was exhausting – I felt full right away, and it was difficult and uncomfortable for me to eat. I ate only about half of what they gave me, and my husband then happily finished the rest. In between meals, they brought me ice cream and juice, and I loved that.

In the afternoon, my stomach started hurting, and I complained about it to the nurse. With a stethoscope she listened to my belly, told me that my stomach was bloated with gas, and she started giving me Metamucil.

They kept doing finger sticks all day long, sticking a needle into the edges of my fingertips, to check my blood glucose level. The finger sticks hurt, and I started dreading them.

In the evening, my husband went home, promising to be back again the next morning.

The day passed in a changing kaleidoscope of food, sleep, nurses, needles, breathing exercises, coughing, and the beeping of monitors. Things settled down more at night, and I dozed on and off throughout the night.

11

COMPETITION AND EXERCISES

The following day, Sunday, June 19, one of the nurses gave me a sponge bath, which felt really good. She then had me brush my teeth by myself over a plastic basin while sitting up in bed. Moving my arm to do that was awkward and uncomfortable, but I did it as well as I could.

In the morning, my husband came to visit, and it was such a joy to see him.

This day I ate a greater amount of my food, and I felt more alert. I only dozed a little in bed, and most of the day I sat in the chair. A few times I stood up and took several steps to try to get my strength back. However, I was extremely weak and unsteady, and I felt very out of it. I could not walk more than a few feet at a time.

Respiratory therapy came and gave me some breathing treatments to help loosen up the congestion in my lungs and help me cough it up. The treatments were wonderful, and I loved them. They put a mask of warm, steamy air over my face, and it was soothing. It felt like being in a sauna. I was then taken off the oxygen.

Lab personnel kept trying to draw blood and could not find a good vein, as my veins kept collapsing or blowing, and their efforts left behind huge purple bruises.

The nurses did more finger sticks to check my glucose level. All day long, I received tons of sticks and punctures and bruises, and I hated all of it.

Across the ICU was an older male patient, probably in his 70s, and I could look into his room from my room. My husband told me that this man had had the same surgery as me, on the same day as me, just before my surgery. *We were buddies!*

I could see him standing up, holding his red heart pillow, and rocking back and forth. That got my competitive spirit going, and it motivated me to try harder. If he could stand up and rock, then I could, too.

It felt good to move, and I stood up and rocked for a little bit, taking tiny steps, wanting to keep up with that man. However, I felt extremely weak and could not do very much or for very long. *Why could that man move and do more than I could?* A few times I stood up and tried keeping up with him, but I did not have the strength or stamina.

Later I found out that the man had had a blood transfusion, and that's why he felt a little stronger than I did. I was told that I did not have a transfusion because my blood loss was not quite enough to require one. But it was borderline, and I had lost enough blood that I was now anemic, which contributed to why I felt so weak and had such a low energy level.

In the afternoon, when my husband and I were alone in the room, I asked him to wash my hair. It had been a few days, and my hair and scalp felt yucky to me. I was desperate to have my hair shampooed, and my husband agreed to help me.

Standing up from the chair, I shuffled over to the sink at the side of the room. There was a small shampoo bottle in the little attached bathroom, and I handed that to Dumitru, along with a cup so that he could rinse my hair.

Bending forward, I stuck my head into the sink right next to the faucet. After wetting my hair, Dumitru added shampoo and lathered it up. *Oh, that felt so good.* Then he used the cup to scoop water over my hair to rinse it.

It was hard to get enough water in the cup to rinse all the shampoo out of my hair, and it was a tiny sink. After trying to rinse my hair for a while and getting out most of the shampoo, we finally gave up. It was good enough, and I felt much better than I did before, even with a little shampoo left in my hair.

While sitting down in the chair with my soaking wet hair, I saw that we had made a mess – water and suds were everywhere, all over the sink and dripping onto the floor. It made me laugh, and I also felt a little guilty, since I knew that someone had to clean that up.

Dumitru towel-dried my hair and then combed it for me. That felt so much better – I now felt less sick and a lot more normal.

After resting for a bit, and seeing that other man walking around, I decided to try going for a short walk. Holding my heart pillow, we ventured outside my room for a slow shuffle around the ICU, and then came back. Feeling weak and exhausted, I gratefully sat back down in the chair to rest.

That evening, a nurse took out my catheter. Up until that point, I didn't even realize that I had a catheter or that I never had to go to the bathroom. But now I would need to get up and walk to the bathroom whenever I needed to go.

On my first trip to the bathroom, I saw some blood and was concerned. *Why was I bleeding? Did I have my period?* I expressed my concerns to the nurse, but she told me no, it's normal, it is from the catheter, and not to worry about it.

On Monday, June 20, I was moved up to a private room, and I was told that I would be discharged the next day. *What? After just having open-heart surgery a few days ago, they're already sending me home?*

Feeling incredibly weak, I was comforted by the fact that I was being monitored and was surrounded by nurses in a medical setting. I did not feel ready to be sent home. However, I also hated all the tubes and wires all over me, and I looked forward to having those removed.

A young man from physical therapy came up and gave me some exercises to do. While standing up and holding onto a chair or table, I had to move my legs around to help build up my strength and stamina.

First I had to stand up on my tippy-toes, then rock back on my heels, and go back and forth, doing that a few times. Then I had to bring one knee up and kick forward, lower it, and then raise my leg out to the side. And I also had to do all of that with the other leg. Then I had to repeat all of that multiple times.

It was uncomfortable, and I felt weak, but I did whatever he told me to do. He told me that this was important to get my muscle strength back. He told me that I needed to do all of these exercises a few times every day.

So throughout the rest of that day, I got out of bed, walked around my new room, looked out the window, and did my leg exercises. That actually felt good, and it helped me to feel more normal, although I still felt very weak.

Every hour, hugging tightly to my pillow to help with the intense agony, I also continued to do my breathing and coughing exercises. I desperately hoped that those would soon get easier and less painful.

The lab technician came up to draw my blood, and this time I refused. I had been getting too many bruises and hematomas from them, and I didn't think I needed that anymore. If I was going home the next day anyway, what was the point?

"No," I told the tech. "No more needle sticks."

"But I have an order to draw blood."

"No," I repeated. "No more."

"Are you refusing?"

"Yes," I answered.

The lab tech made a note and then left, without sticking me. I was glad. *Good riddance!*

12

Going Home

Tuesday arrived, and I knew I was getting discharged that day. I had mixed feelings. I felt so exhausted, feeble, scared, and vulnerable, and I did not feel ready to go home. But I was also so sick of all the tubes, wires, needles, monitors, and being hooked up to machines. It would be nice to leave all that behind and be free and unencumbered.

After breakfast, a nurse came to my room and said that I was now cleared to go home, and I could leave whenever I wanted. She removed all the tubes, wires, and IVs, and I was now free.

I called my husband and told him to come get me, and I packed up my few belongings. While waiting for Dumitru to arrive, I walked around the room and did my leg stretches and the painful breathing exercises.

Once my husband showed up at my room, a nurse took me by wheelchair to the main entrance of the hospital. Dumitru went to get the car while the nurse and I waited outside the front entrance, and within a few minutes, he drove the car right up in front of us. Clutching my heart pillow, I carefully got up from the wheelchair. After thanking the nurse, I gingerly got into the car. I hooked the seatbelt, but I held it at least a few inches away from my chest.

The drive home was incredibly scary for me. Every bump in the road felt jarring and uncomfortable, and I felt so highly fragile. I felt like I could split open with any shake of the car.

"Slow down!" I yelled after every slight curve or bump in the road.

"I'm only going 30," Dumitru replied. Despite knowing that he was driving slowly, it still felt fast and dangerous to me.

Staying on side streets the whole way, he drove cautiously, way under the speed limit. Still feeling scared and so incredibly vulnerable, I certainly did not feel ready to be in a car, or even out of the hospital. For the entire drive home, I felt like I could break or shatter at any moment.

I felt like I still needed to be surrounded by doctors and nurses. *What if the heart valve stopped working? What if blood started spurting from my chest? Who would help me?*

A few blocks from our house, my husband pulled into the local Auto Club office to get a disabled-parking placard for me.

"Let's get this taken care of while you're here in the car, in case you need to come in," he said. Taking the paperwork, he went into the Auto Club office, while I waited in the car, feeling vaguely anxious and unsettled. It did not take long, and within five minutes he came back out, holding the placard. Feeling relieved, we then went home.

I had been discharged with a set of instructions – various things that I could or could not do, such as not lifting more than five pounds the first month. I was also given a list of exercises that I needed to do every day, prescriptions to fill, and booklets and pamphlets to read.

It was difficult for me to concentrate or focus on anything, and I put everything in a pile on the counter and sat down at the kitchen table, clutching my red heart pillow.

It felt good to be home, but I felt incredibly vulnerable, weak, and exhausted.

"I'm going to run to the drug store and fill your prescription," Dumitru told me. "Are you okay by yourself for a little bit?"

"Yes, I'm okay, just scared," I told him.

He hesitated and said, "I'll be back as soon as I can." He then left, and I heard him start the car.

I felt untethered, like I was floating free somewhere, no longer connected to medical help and support. No one was monitoring everything and ready to jump in with medical expertise, if needed. *Was it really okay for me to be on my own so soon?*

Remaining seated at the kitchen table, I waited for Dumitru to return. He was back in about 20 minutes, and I felt better having him home with me.

"I dropped off the prescription," he told me. "It will be ready in about an hour, so I'll go back after lunch to pick it up."

"Okay," I answered. "I feel so weak."

"Don't forget that's also because you're anemic from so much blood loss," he answered. "Let me see your hands."

I held out my hands, and he turned them over to see my palms. My palms were almost white, with barely a trace of color in them. Dumitru held his palms next to mine – and his were rosy pink. What a huge difference!

It was now almost noon, and we needed to eat lunch. I felt out of it and helpless, unable to do anything. "I'll go out and get lunch for us," Dumitru offered. "What would you like?"

After thinking for a minute, I looked up at him. "Since I'm so anemic, maybe chopped liver would be good," I told him. That had also been a childhood favorite of mine, and I looked forward to that.

Dumitru agreed, and he ran out to a local deli to get lunch. In addition to the chopped liver, he brought back matzo ball soup and a three-bean salad.

My husband put the soup in a small bowl, and small portions of the rest of the food on a plate for me. It was still difficult for me to eat much, and I found eating to be very tiring.

"It's too much," I complained, picking at the food. But it tasted really good, and I tried to eat as much as I could.

The effort to eat completely exhausted me, and when I finished, I desperately needed to sleep. Afraid to lie down, I looked around to see where I could sit. The couch looked too difficult for me to get in and out of without using my arms or hands, so I chose to sit upright in the recliner, holding onto my red heart pillow.

Dumitru cleaned up after lunch, he ran back to the drug store to pick up my prescription, and I dozed in the recliner.

In the afternoon I got on the computer and sent an e-mail to my family back east, letting them know that I was alive, I was home, and I was okay. That left me fatigued, and I did not have the focus or stamina to do more than that.

Later that afternoon I realized that although I was weak and tired, I did not need much care – what I needed most was rest. So I relaxed, releasing some of the fear.

Dumitru had set up a metal folding chair in the living room for me to sit on, which gave really firm back support and felt stable. I sat on that for a while but, without any armrests, I was afraid of falling off the chair when I got sleepy, and I went back to the recliner.

I did my leg stretches and then the breathing exercises. It felt good to move, and I walked through the rooms of the house again, carrying the heart pillow.

That first day home was scary and unsettling. Not yet feeling ready to go outside, I stayed in the house. I did very little as I did not have the focus or the energy to read or even watch TV. In a blurry haze, the day passed quickly.

Brushing my teeth before bed was uncomfortable. I still felt weak, it was difficult standing for very long, and the arm movement to brush my teeth was awkward and made my chest ache. I couldn't wait to finish, and I hoped that this would quickly get easier. However, once it was done, I felt much better.

That first night, afraid to lie down in bed or have to struggle to get all the way down and all the way up by myself without using my arms, I decided to just sleep in the recliner. So I got comfortable, my husband put a light blanket over me, and I dozed there, on and off, all night.

The nurses had warned me that it was normal to have nightmares after this type of surgery and not to let it bother me. They sure were right. I had horrible nightmares that first night – about bizarre aliens who came here from outer space, chomped at my flesh, grabbed at my brain, and took over my body. I woke up in the middle of the night shaking with fear, afraid to go back to sleep. I tried to stay awake for a little bit so that I would not go right back into that same nightmare. Then, exhausted, I finally fell back asleep.

13

The First Shower

My back ached when I woke up the next morning, and I realized that sleeping all night long in the recliner was not good for my back. Dumitru said he would help to arrange a wedge of pillows in bed for me the next night, so that I could be somewhat reclining, and at least be in my own bed. That sounded good to me.

First thing in the morning, my chest was painful and achy. I took my prescribed Vicodin, and that took the edge off it. I did not want to become addicted to pain pills, so I wanted to take as few as possible while still being comfortable. But I knew that for at least the first week, I needed to take them as prescribed, whenever I needed them. That day, I took Vicodin around the clock.

Dumitru had to help me dress, and he would for at least a full week, since I could not bend forward, reach, or pull. He helped me put on my underwear, shorts, socks, shoes, and a t-shirt. He tied the laces on my shoes differently than I do, and they looked funny to me. Over that first week, sometimes he would tie the laces too tight, and sometimes too loose. I often yelled at him about the laces and told him that he was doing them wrong, and we both would laugh. However, I knew that he was doing his best, and I was very grateful that he was doing them for me at all. I looked forward to the time when I could dress myself without assistance.

Although Dumitru stayed home with me my first day home, on the second day he needed to go back to work. He dressed me, fed me breakfast, cleaned up, made sure I was settled comfortably in the recliner, and then he went to work.

This day I felt a little better and a bit more alert, but I was still weak and could not do much. I dozed, walked around the house, sent a couple e-mails, and then slept in the recliner some more.

I still did not have the focus or stamina to read. After putting on the television, I quickly found that even watching TV demanded more focus than I was capable of, and I turned it off.

Later in the morning I decided to go outside for a few minutes. I felt nervous leaving the security of the house, even though I was only going into the back yard. I opened the slider and walked down the two small steps to the back patio.

Wow – fresh air. That felt wonderful. Avoiding the uneven grass, I walked around on the patio and concrete path, enjoying the warm breezes and sunshine. Being out there felt like a huge, thrilling adventure. I walked around, back and forth between the patio and walkway, holding that red heart pillow to my chest. There was no chair out there that would be easy for me to sit in, so I just walked for a few minutes, feeling the fresh air on my face, and then I went back inside. That was enough, but it felt amazing.

Gingerly walking into the den, I became aware of a powerful, booming heartbeat. I could feel it pounding in my chest, BOOM-BOOM, BOOM-BOOM, over and over. I could hear it echoing and reverberating in my ears – BOOM-BOOM, BOOM-BOOM, loud and intense. And I could also see it – my vision pulsed with it, contracting and narrowing into a smaller, muted gray with each BOOM-BOOM, and then releasing back to wide, full color vision in between the heartbeats.

Why was my heartbeat so intense and powerful? Then it hit me that my heart had been working much harder than normal before the surgery, trying to squeeze blood through a faulty, constricted valve. It seemed that my heart was still trying to do that, not yet realizing that it didn't need to work so hard anymore.

Dumitru came home for lunch and fed me, and that was so comforting. He gave me more of the matzo ball soup, chopped liver, and the three-bean salad, and I was still only able to eat a small portion. Then I was exhausted. I went back to the recliner and slept, and Dumitru went back to work.

After dozing in the recliner, I walked around the house, in and out of the rooms, and I sent another e-mail to my family back east. I did my leg stretches and my breathing and coughing exercises, and then I sat down and dozed again.

That evening I asked my husband to put a small folding chair outside on the patio for me. He set that up right away, and I looked forward to sitting there the next day.

After dinner, I told Dumitru that I wanted to take a shower. I had been told that it was okay to get my chest wet, but I could not soak it – no bathtub or pool, and no direct spray. *How could I do this?* I did not yet feel strong enough to stand up in a shower and take care of that myself, especially on a slippery wet floor.

We decided that the easiest way was for me to sit on a sturdy chair in the bathtub in our guest bathroom, and have Dumitru help wash me. He placed a shower chair in the empty bathtub, and he hooked up a sprayer that I could easily use. My husband then carefully helped me into the tub and onto the chair. Then he started the water, making sure to aim the sprayer away from me.

First Dumitru washed my hair and rinsed it, and that felt so amazingly good. Then, still sitting on the plastic chair, I was able to soap up and rinse off my body, being careful to not spray my chest directly. For the first time since the surgery, I felt really clean, and that felt incredible.

During that shower I discovered that they had shaved my entire pubic area. That was a surprise – no one had mentioned that that would happen, and I did not understand why that was needed.

Then Dumitru helped me get out of the tub, and he carefully dried me off with a soft towel. The entire process was a huge, time-consuming ordeal, but I felt so good afterwards.

Before bedtime, Dumitru set up a foam wedge on my side of the bed, and he added couch pillows to it, so that I would be half sitting up in bed. But I wasn't sure how to get in, since I could not use my hands.

I carefully sat on the edge of the bed and crossed my arms over my chest. Dumitru helped support me as I leaned back into the pillows, and then he lifted my legs up onto the bed. Next, he placed a large pillow under my knees, which felt wonderful. I was now comfortable, but I could not move, and I would not be able to roll over or change position.

He then put the red heart pillow on a chair, and he moved it next to my bed so that I could reach it if I needed it.

"What if I need to go to the bathroom during the night?" I asked him.

"Then wake me up, any time," he said earnestly.

And I did. I was not sleeping very well, maybe only one or two hours at a time. In the middle of the night, I needed to pee. Somehow my husband sensed that I was awake.

"Are you okay?" he asked.

"I need to go to the bathroom," I told him.

He jumped out of bed and was quickly at my side to help me. He supported my back and helped me sit up, as I moved my legs over the side. Once I was sitting, I could then stand up by myself, and I made my way to the bathroom, my husband hovering nearby in case I needed help. When I was done, my husband helped me back into bed.

"I can't see a clock," I told him. My clock was on my nightstand behind me, and I could not twist around to see it.

"We'll put another clock on your dresser tomorrow, so you can see it from sitting up in bed," he promised.

14

Sneezes and Visitors

My chest was again very achy when I woke up the next day. Dumitru helped me out of bed, as that was still very awkward for me to do on my own. Brushing my teeth was getting a little easier.

My husband helped me dress, and then he fed me. I took Vicodin with breakfast and waited for relief from the pain while Dumitru cleaned up.

After my husband left for work, I went out in the back yard, and it again felt like a huge adventure. I smiled, looking around at the green grass, flowering bushes, and the leaves on the trees gently fluttering in the soft breeze. It felt so good to be outside, as though I was once again part of life.

Sitting in the sturdy folding chair that my husband had put on the patio for me the previous evening, I relaxed, for a few moments feeling a little better and not quite so fragile. I absolutely cherished the simple act of just sitting outside in the fresh air like a normal person.

It suddenly hit me that I wasn't hearing, feeling, or seeing my heart pound anymore, so I knew that my heart was relaxing back into a more gentle, normal rhythm, which was really good news.

Feeling a little stronger, I spent a bit more time walking and doing my leg exercises. And, knowing how important it was, I also did all my breathing and coughing exercises, clutching the red pillow to my chest to help alleviate some of the intense pain.

My husband came home again at lunch to feed me. Having run out of the deli food, he made me a small sandwich, promising that he would go back to the deli that evening and get more food. As usual, I felt exhausted after lunch, and when my husband went back to work, I sat in the recliner and dozed.

The doorbell rang in the afternoon while I was resting comfortably in the recliner. *Who could that be? Maybe someone was delivering flowers.*

I got up and slowly made my way to the front door. A young man in a uniform was at the door, and there was a van in the street. "Are you Lynn? We have a delivery here for a wheelchair."

"Yes," I answered, opening the door all the way. He went back to the van, unloaded the wheelchair, and brought it to the front door. After showing me the order, he said the wheelchair was a loan and would be picked up again in six weeks.

When I finished signing the paperwork, he brought in and set up the wheelchair. I liked the chair right away – it was very comfortable and offered a lot of support and mobility for me. I knew this would really be of immense assistance when we needed to go anywhere.

After he left, I went back outside on the patio, and I again sat in the sturdy folding chair. *How incredibly amazing it was to be alive and to be able to sit out there in the fresh air.* Closing my eyes, it almost felt like I was an average, healthy person, simply relaxing in the back yard.

Later that afternoon, I took four Advil in place of the Vicodin, and that worked for a while. But soon the achiness grew into a more powerful pain, and I again took Vicodin. However, I knew that I was beginning to wean off the stronger medication, and I was glad.

Coughing at any time, whether with or without the machine, was extremely painful, and holding that pillow tightly to my chest made a huge difference and made it tolerable.

Sneezing, however, was a different matter. Thankfully, I did not sneeze the first couple days I was home. Then, late that afternoon, all of a sudden – *SNEEZE!* I froze in absolute shock, in intense, horrific agony. I sat there, mouth open, paralyzed, unable to move for quite a few seconds. The pain hung on and lingered for a few minutes before dissipating. That was absolutely the most intense pain I had ever felt, and I did not want to *ever* sneeze again.

I sent a few e-mails, walked around the house, and then found that I was now able to watch TV for short periods of time. That was relaxing and felt good, as long as I did not sneeze.

At night, I told my husband that I was sitting too far up in bed and needed to lie back further. He removed a few pillows so that I would be lying a little lower in the bed. After helping me get into bed, I found that lying down a little flatter felt much better. The new clock that Dumitru had placed on my dresser was easily visible, and that was very helpful.

Waking up the following day, I was again very achy. It seemed that the mornings were the most painful time for me, so for the next few days I continued to take Vicodin first thing in the morning, and I started switching to Advil in the afternoons, slowly weaning myself off the Vicodin.

Feeling a little stronger that day, and buoyed by my thrill of being in the back yard for the past two days, I decided to try walking up the street in front of the house. Holding tightly onto my red heart pillow, and making sure I took my key, I ventured out the front door.

I felt a bit hesitant and afraid. *Was I strong enough to do this?* Taking little baby steps, I slowly shuffled up to the house next door. I was thrilled. And that was enough. I did not yet want to be far from home and security, and I turned and slowly shuffled back. Once I safely got back inside, I relaxed, proud of that small feat.

The first few days home, I could only speak very softly. I could not project my voice, and I did not have the stamina or the lung power to speak on the telephone. Ignoring the phone when it rang, I let my husband handle all phone calls.

I also did not want any visitors. Not only was it difficult to speak, but I did not have the strength to keep up a conversation, entertain anyone, or act happy and social.

My parents had finally returned from their trip, and they called and asked to talk to me. Dumitru spoke to them, explained that it was too difficult for me to talk on the phone, and he told them about my surgery. They wanted to come see me right away, but Dumitru put them off for a couple days, telling them that I was still too weak, and to come on Saturday when he would be home.

Trying to make it easier on me during their upcoming visit and hopefully rest my voice and not tax myself too much, I typed out a page full of information as to what was wrong with my heart, what was done, and how I was feeling. Trying to anticipate what questions my parents would ask, I incorporated as much as I could onto my typed page.

My parents arrived on Saturday afternoon, bustling in with nervous energy. Not being a big cook, my mother brought us raw food – chicken, broccoli stalks, and two sweet potatoes. Thanking her, we put the food aside.

We sat in the living room, and my parents asked non-stop questions, their voices loud and insistent, filled with concern and anxiety. I handed them my typed sheet, hoping that would answer everything, so that I could avoid talking and conserve my strength. But they simply glanced at it and then continued with their questions, barely giving me time to answer.

As they continued bombarding me, I felt an increasing level of anxiety and pressure in my chest. It was difficult to respond to all their questions, as I could not project my voice enough to be heard, and they kept interrupting me.

Then I showed them my surgical scar, and I watched their mouths drop open while shock and horror showed on their faces.

We talked a little more, and my strength and stamina started rapidly fading. I did the best I could, and I hoped that they would soon leave. After about an hour, I told them that I was too tired and needed to rest, and that I could not talk any more. They said they understood, they wished me well, and they finally went home.

After they were gone, it felt so good to be left with silence and peace. Thoroughly exhausted and wiped out, I dozed for the rest of the day.

The next day I felt stronger, and I looked forward to again walking outside. Venturing out into the fresh air, I shuffled all the way past three houses. Then feeling uneasy and too far from home and safety, I turned and slowly made my way back home.

Later that morning I needed to sneeze. Over the past few days, I had been doing whatever I could to ward it off and stop it. I wiggled my nose, exhaled through my nose, touched my nose, and did anything possible that would interrupt and stop the progression of a sneeze.

Most of the time it worked and prevented a sneeze. But today it wasn't enough, and I felt a sneeze building. I grabbed my pillow, pressed it desperately into my sternum, and sneezed. *SHOCK!* Horrific agony shot through my chest, bringing tears to my eyes. It took a full minute or two before the pain dissipated and I could relax again. It was torture, and I dreaded sneezing more than anything.

That afternoon, while researching online about open-heart surgery, I found a support group for those who had been through a valve replacement. The group seemed very supportive, and I quickly joined, feeling excited to belong.

They discussed and shared many difficulties, questions, issues, and concerns related to heart valve replacement and the surgery – and there was always a lot of help from the other members. I felt comfortable right away and joined in the conversations.

I had very few questions myself; most of my posts were helping others with kindness and compassion, giving support where needed, and helping people feel comfortable with their decisions and with where they were in their recovery process.

Feeling excited and empowered, I really looked forward to being more active in this online support group.

15

MILESTONES

Knowing that walking was good for me, I wanted to push myself and walk more than I had been. I decided to walk at least half-way up the block. Feeling stronger and walking a little faster now, I fairly easily walked about half-way up the street and then past another two houses. *Enough,* I told myself, and I turned around and walked back home. It was becoming more comfortable to walk, but I didn't want to be too far from home yet.

It felt good to be up and moving, and I was not sleeping as much anymore. I now had more stamina and could focus more, so I spent more time on the computer, and I started reading.

I was very conscientious about doing my leg stretches and my breathing exercises, which were still painful. I was also still trying very hard not to sneeze.

The following day I wanted to walk even farther, and I made it all the way up the block, almost reaching the end, but I was afraid to go all the way around the block. *What if I got in trouble or needed to sit down? What if I felt too weak or something was wrong? I'd be too far from home.* So a bit worried, I turned around and went back down the street to home. Maybe tomorrow I would go all the way around the block.

The next day, now a full week home, I decided that this was the day to go all the way around the block. I clutched my red heart pillow and started up the street. I felt like I was walking faster now, although I'm sure it was still slow compared to how I used to walk when I was healthy.

Feeling strong and more comfortable, I easily reached the end of the street. *Now what? Should I go all the way around?* I knew that once I walked around the corner, I would reach the point of no return and have to continue all the way around the entire block.

A jolt of fear went through me as I considered continuing around the block. In addition to my previous concerns of not feeling well or needing to sit, I now also worried that I might simply be too weak to make it all the way around the block. *And what would I do if I fell? What if the valve stopped working? What if my heart gave out?*

Then again, I was healing and getting stronger, and I knew that I needed to walk more. *Was today the day that I walked all the way around the block?* I decided to do it.

I continued walking around the corner, past the point of no return, and then down the next street. Now I had to keep going, and I felt nervous – it felt like I was a long way from home. If I was in trouble for any reason, I was out there on my own.

Holding onto my pillow, I simply kept walking, one foot in front of the other, short little baby steps, all the way down the other street. After about ten minutes, I reached the end of that street, turned the corner, and then I was getting closer to home. Now I wasn't so scared anymore, and I could more calmly walk the last stretch. *I could do this.*

Once I got back inside the house, I relaxed – it felt so good to be home again and feel safe. I felt much better after that walk, and I realized that going around the block was not as hard as I thought it would be. It might have taken me 25 minutes or so to walk the half mile around the whole block, but I could now do it.

I was proud of myself. *A new milestone!* I was determined to do that every day from that point forward.

And I did – from that day on, I went around the entire block every day. And each day I could walk a little faster, and it got a little easier and more comfortable.

~

During the second week home, I took Advil most of the time, and I only took Vicodin when I really needed it. By the end of the second week, I was taking only Advil.

That week I started taking showers on my own. Dumitru put the shower chair into our master bath shower stall, hooked up the hose sprayer, and I was now able to wash myself without any help. It was still awkward to dry myself off with a towel, but I did the best I could. It didn't matter to me if some areas were not dried very well, I was now more independent, even if a bit wet, and that felt great. *It was another milestone.*

I also started dressing myself, but I had to do so very slowly and cautiously so that I did not strain myself. But I was thrilled that I could now do that by myself. *Another milestone.*

Most of the time, especially when I was home, I did not wear a bra, as the band would uncomfortably press on my chest. The few times that I did, I found that I needed to put a sock in the front under the band to protect my sensitive incision scar. But I preferred as much as possible to not wear one.

I also found that cold air, or even a cool breeze, made my chest ache. In order to avoid that intense achiness, I needed to keep the area around my breastbone warm. When I was in bed, resting in a chair, walking, or in a car with the air conditioning on, I always grabbed a blanket or sweatshirt, and I made sure that my chest was covered and kept warm.

In the online support group for those who had valve replacement surgery, I was particularly interested in reading the comments from those who had chosen the different types of valves. *What were the experiences and thoughts of those who had chosen the mechanical valve versus the tissue valve? Did I make the right decision?* I searched the posted comments, looking for confirmation that my decision had been a good one.

From those who had the mechanical valve, I read with great interest about constantly hearing the clicks, and also about problems with Coumadin, the blood thinner. Some had problems and issues with that, and some didn't. They also commented about needing to constantly get their blood drawn to check the levels of Coumadin.

There were not as many comments from those who had the tissue valve, and there were no problems or issues that I read about, so it seemed that I had made the right choice.

Then I started noticing that there was one person in the group who appeared to be very negative. He was having a difficult time with various complications from his own surgery, and he was very vocal about it. He also constantly attacked people for their opinions, especially those who had chosen a tissue valve or who were happy with their progress.

He kept telling the group over and over that those who chose a tissue valve instead of a mechanical valve were idiots, and that they were stupid to choose to go through another horrendous surgery, and anyone who was happy after that surgery was living in a fantasy world.

At first, I ignored all his comments, but he kept going on and on, putting down those of us who chose a tissue valve. It made me very uncomfortable, and it made me doubt my decision. *Was he right? Did I choose the wrong valve? Did I make a mistake? Was it wrong to knowingly choose to have to go through another surgery?* Awful feelings of self-doubt churned in the pit of my stomach.

Finally, I decided to stand up to this negative person. I told him to stop putting down the people who chose a tissue valve, and I explained that we all need to feel good about our decisions. I told him that even if we were wrong, we couldn't go back and un-do our previous choice, so we needed to feel good about where we were.

But he didn't let up. He continued to berate us, and his comments upset me. Finally having enough, I posted that this person should be stopped from posting his negative attacks, or he should simply be removed from the group.

That did not go over well. Although I did not know it at the time, it turned out that this negative person was one of the administrators and had been there for many years. Not only that, but others in the group now thought that I was a bully who had previously created trouble a year or two earlier, and who had now returned under a new name to infiltrate the group and create new problems. Mistaken about my identity, they now started personally attacking *me*.

Trying to explain that I was not who they thought I was, I told them that I was new, and to look at all my previous posts, which were all positive and supportive. But they didn't believe me, and they continued to gang up on me and relentlessly attack me, calling me a rowdy no-good spy who only wanted to cause trouble.

Feeling horribly vulnerable and still in a very weak and needy state, I could not tolerate their belligerence, and I dissolved into tears. Their relentless and cruel attacks made me feel very depressed and let down, and I cried on and off for days. Not only had I lost my support group, but I was now the target of their vicious verbal aggression, and it was from the very group I had been reaching out to for comfort and support. I could not stop crying.

I sent a private e-mail to the owner of the site, who sent back an apology to me, but he did nothing more about it, and I still felt very depressed. I stayed away from the group for a few days, and then I checked back a few days later to see what they were talking about, thinking that maybe it had all blown over. However, I saw that they were patting each other on the back and congratulating themselves for getting rid of me, now convinced that they were correct and that I was their previous tormentor.

That really hurt me, and I got very upset and cried again. I decided to never go back there, and I dropped out of the group completely. After a few days, the emotional hurt began dissipating, and I started feeling better. I missed having a support group, but it was not worth being the target of their attacks.

16

DRIVING

At two weeks post-op, using my wheelchair, I went to Dr. Soldano, the cardiac surgeon, for a check-up. While sitting in the waiting room, the receptionist gave me some forms to fill out. As I was filling them out, I noticed medical reports behind the forms. Curious, I looked at them to see what they contained. As I read some of the notes and information, I was shocked. "Patient is in congestive heart failure," I read, feeling a lump in my throat.

We were shortly called into an examination room, and within a few minutes, the cardiac surgeon joined us.

Once Dr. Soldano examined me, he told me that everything was healing well. He showed me a sample tissue valve similar to what was put in my heart, and he displayed an x-ray of my chest which showed the metal wires holding my breastbone together. All of that left me feeling a bit queasy and unnerved.

The doctor told me to do some upper body stretches so that I wouldn't get too stiff, and he demonstrated a few stretches that I could do, which I did along with him.

He then said that I could drive a car whenever it felt comfortable to do so. He also reminded me that for the first month, I could not lift more than five pounds, and not more than ten pounds the second month.

I did not yet feel quite ready to drive, so I decided to let that go for at least another week. But in the meantime, I added the upper body stretches to my routine with the leg exercises. With all those stretches and exercises, and with now walking faster and farther, up to a mile each day, I was noticeably gaining strength and stamina.

There were days when I felt much better, and days when I felt like I would never feel good again. But I knew that overall I was improving, and I needed to simply keep going and allow myself to recover, however long it took.

All that week, I thought about driving. *When should I try? Could I drive yet? Was I ready?* I wasn't sure, and it did not yet feel right.

One week after my visit to the cardiac surgeon, about three weeks post-op, I decided to try. Slowly and carefully I got in my car, not putting any weight on my hands. *But how could I use a seatbelt which would press across my chest?* I pulled the belt across me and, while holding it away from my chest, I buckled it. *Now what?*

I put the heart pillow across my chest, but it was too bulky to get the seatbelt over that. I would need to find a smaller pillow. I got out of the car, went back in the house, and chose a smaller pillow from the couch. *Would that work?*

Getting back in the car, I tried again. This time, holding the smaller pillow in place, I put the seatbelt over that. The pressure of that on my chest was a bit painful, but I didn't think I was doing any damage. Figuring that my chest was just very sensitive, I tried to ignore it.

Sitting there in my car gave me an amazing sense of independence, and now I wanted to drive. First I decided to just go around the block and see how that felt. I slowly backed out of the garage and down the driveway, and I quickly realized that it was way too difficult and painful to twist around to look behind me. But I knew that I could use mirrors and be really careful.

Very slowly, checking my mirrors, I backed out all the way into the street. Then I put the car in drive and cautiously crept forward. Being able to drive felt so empowering!

I drove slowly around the block, and then pulled back up the driveway and into the garage. That was enough for one day. But it helped me feel that if I needed to, I could make it a few blocks to the grocery store. *Another milestone.*

That weekend Dumitru told me that he wanted to take me out to dinner. I was a bit excited but also nervous – *how could we do this?*

We took the wheelchair and went to our favorite Italian restaurant. Although I was apprehensive, the wheelchair made it not only much easier but also somewhat fun, as I was wheeled through the restaurant to our table.

When we looked up from our menus, we saw that our waiter was someone who had waited on us many times before, and we recognized each other right away.

"Hey, I haven't seen you in a while," he said to us as he placed glasses of water on the table. "How have you been?"

"I had open-heart surgery."

"What? Are you okay?"

"I'm still recovering. Here, look at my scar," I said, pulling my shirt down to show him the top of the scar.

The waiter's mouth fell open. "Oh God, I'm so sorry," he said.

We ordered our meals, and the waiter soon brought steaming hot plates to our table. The food was delicious, although I could not eat as much as I used to, and he boxed up most of my meal for me to take home.

I enjoyed being in the restaurant, but I also felt a bit uneasy around that many people and so much activity.

After our waiter cleared the plates, he returned shortly and placed a dish of Tiramisu on the table.

"We didn't order this," I told him.

"I know. This is on me – no charge. I hope you heal completely and stay healthy."

Tears filled my eyes as we ate the sweet, delicate dessert. We left him a huge tip, and then Dumitru wheeled me out to the car, as I wiggled my feet with nervous delight. The whole dinner felt like a big adventure, and although I felt uncomfortable with all the hustle and bustle, I also looked forward to having dinner out again soon.

The wheelchair came in handy numerous times, and I was so thankful to have it. It helped me smoothly and comfortably get to medical appointments, go through various stores, and go to restaurants, which we started doing more often. It made much easier what would have been daunting and difficult excursions.

A few days later, I realized that we needed a few items from the supermarket, and I didn't want to make my husband go after work if I could take care of it by myself. Feeling stronger and also somewhat scared, I got back into my car. I put the small pillow on my chest and the seatbelt over that. It was still painful, but it was tolerable.

A bit nervous, I carefully backed out into the street. Driving very cautiously, checking my mirrors constantly, I slowly drove the few blocks to the grocery store, and I parked in a handicapped spot near the entrance.

I carefully got out of the car and slowly walked into the supermarket. Near the entrance were those little electric scooters with an attached basket that I could use, and I was so relieved. *Could I figure out how to work it?*

Sitting down in one of them, I read the brief instructions and fiddled with the controls. It wasn't too hard, and I caught on rather quickly. Then I took off.

It was actually fun in that scooter. Wheeling around the first aisle to where I needed to be, I stood up to get what I wanted, put it in the basket, sat back down, and then scooted off again. *I could do this!*

I made my way up and down the aisles, getting everything I needed, and then I headed to the front to check out. Standing up, I put each item, one at a time, on the conveyer belt, and then I sat back down in the scooter.

When they bagged up my purchases, I asked them to please keep the bags very light, and I explained that I had recently had open-heart surgery and could not lift more than five pounds. They did as I requested, and for the first time, I said yes to being helped out to my car. The supermarket clerk loaded everything into the trunk for me, and I thanked him.

Then I drove home. They had done a great job of keeping the bags light, and I made quite a few trips from my car to the kitchen, carrying in one bag at a time.

Wow! I did it! Another milestone.

After that time, if I needed anything heavy, such as a large container of water, I asked someone in the store to load it into the cart for me, and I then had help with bringing it to my car. After getting home, I simply left it in the trunk of my car until Dumitru came home in the evening, and he would then bring it into the house.

At the end of that week we went to Dr. Tillman, the cardiologist, for my one-month post-surgery visit. The wheelchair made it much easier to get around, and I was so glad that we had it. After examining me, the doctor told me that everything looked good, and that I no longer needed to use the breathing machine. *What a relief – I was very glad to stop that!*

Dr. Tillman also emphasized that to prevent having to be opened up again, it was critical that the new valve not become infected. He told me that from now on, before any minor surgery or dental procedure, including routine teeth cleaning, I would need to take antibiotic pills. After making sure that I understood the importance of this, he handed me a prescription for antibiotics to keep on hand so that I would be prepared.

He then asked me how active I was and what my activities were. When he found out that I was still afraid of doing much more than walking and stretching, he told me that I needed help with rehabilitation, and that I needed to go to cardiac rehab. Somewhat reluctantly, with fear bubbling in my belly, I agreed.

Dr. Tillman then took me across the hall from his office, and he gave me a quick tour of the rehab area. It was a modest gym situated in one small square room, but to me it looked like a medieval torture chamber, and I did not at all feel ready for that.

For the next few days, I dreaded going to cardiac rehab. *Was it too much for me? Was it too soon?*

17

Cardiac Rehab

The following Monday, I went to cardiac rehab, and I tentatively entered the small room. Looking around, I saw treadmills, stationary bikes, and various machines along the walls. I noticed that the ages of the patients there ranged from the 30s to the 80s, although most were at the older end.

"Hi, welcome," a woman wearing a pink flowered nursing outfit greeted me with a smile. "I'm Amy, one of the cardiac nurses here. Are you Lynn?"

"Yes," I answered, my stomach in knots.

"Excellent, we've been expecting you. I have your paperwork here, and I just need you to fill out this one form." She handed me a pen and a clipboard holding a form, and I sat down on a nearby bench and filled it out.

After asking me a few more questions, Amy then asked me to step on a scale, and she recorded my weight. She then hooked cardiac wires to my chest and handed me a portable device to clip onto my clothes, so that I would be mobile and the cardiac nurses could constantly monitor my heart.

"For the first week," Amy told me, "we're going to start you with mostly lower body exercises, and just a few easy upper body movements to help you get more of your strength back. Then we'll slowly add more upper body exercises." She paused and pointed at some of the equipment. "The first thing we'll have you do is gentle walking on a treadmill, and we will be constantly monitoring your heart rate and rhythm while you are here."

Feeling intimidated by the array of machines surrounding me, and scared that they would expect too much from me, I meekly listened to Amy's instructions. And still not quite sure if I was even ready for this, I was briefly tempted to walk out.

She started me very slowly – in fact, too slowly. She had me get on a treadmill, and she set the speed at only 1.2 miles per hour. However, I was already walking faster than that on my own at home, and I manually increased the speed on the machine to 1.5. After a few more minutes, I increased it again to 2.0 miles per hour.

After the treadmill, Amy put me on a stationary bicycle for five minutes. Then she gave me three-pound weights and showed me a few exercises to do with those.

Next, she had me stand in a specific position and pull a cord out from a wall and then slowly release it, first with one hand, and then with the other. It looked daunting, but the cords pulled out smoothly and easily, and I did not feel strained.

"Next week," she told me, "we'll have you do more rigorous upper body movements."

By the end of the session, I was feeling good and was looking forward to the next one. Amy removed all the cardiac wires from me and told me that I should come there three times a week, at whatever time was most convenient for me.

As I was leaving, she told me that I should not do anything too strenuous and that I should not yet be driving for a few more weeks. I kept my mouth shut – I did not want to tell her that that's how I was getting there.

Cardiac rehab felt really invigorating. I went there every Monday, Wednesday, and Friday morning, and I was definitely getting stronger and was so glad that I was going.

As soon as I arrived each time, I weighed myself and then got hooked up to the cardiac wires. Then I walked on the treadmill, rode the stationary bike, pulled cords from the wall, lifted small weights, and used my arms to pedal a wheel on a table.

Every so often, Amy added new routines or increased the weights or tension on the machines.

I felt stronger, more powerful, and also much more normal. Without any doubt, I knew that I would not have progressed nearly as fast if I was on my own.

It felt very rewarding as I got more independent. Driving was difficult, as it was still hard to twist all the way around and look behind me, and the pressure of the seatbelt across my chest, even with a pillow under it, was still painful. But I could drive slowly for short distances. I felt comfortable driving to the supermarket, cardiac rehab, and the doctor's office, and that was all I needed for now.

Wherever I went, I kept my heart pillow with me. I actually received many comments about my pillow from other people when I was out somewhere. Most people admired it but had no idea what it was for.

One time, I was in the check-out line at our local Target store, holding onto my red heart pillow like I always did. When I was at the register and paying, the customer behind me tapped me on the shoulder. "I really like your heart pillow. That is so cool," she said. "Where did you get it?"

I smiled at her. "I got it from the hospital where I had open-heart surgery," I explained. "I am still recovering. See – here's my scar," I added, pulling my blouse down a little so she could see the huge, red, ropy scar in the middle of my chest. Her face puckered up in horror. "I'm so sorry," she said.

I was actually proud of my scar and enjoyed showing it to people – in stores and in restaurants. The scar was thick, with a lot of keloid tissue. I was hoping that in time, the scar would diminish and not be quite so massive. But for now, it didn't bother me at all.

After six weeks, they came and picked up the wheelchair. Although I was now using it less often, I wished I could have kept it – it was a nice security blanket to have, but I understood that it was not mine to keep.

That week I found myself getting depressed. My energy level was low, I felt tired most of the time, and it felt like I would never feel strong or normal again. It felt like I had been beaten up and that my body was recovering from a huge trauma, which it actually was. I realized that it would take a long time to fully recover, and that I needed to just keep going.

It then hit me that I was moving through a grieving process, through all the typical stages of grief, including shock and depression. It made sense, as this was a serious loss of health and of perceived health, and it was a severe trauma for my body. So I knew that the grieving process was good for me.

I had been scheduled to return to work after eight weeks, but I did not yet feel ready to plunge back into the working world with all the demands of a job. I asked Dr. Moore to request another two weeks for my recovery, telling him that I still felt too weak, and he agreed. He signed the forms and said that I was to remain on disability an additional two weeks, and I was to return to work after ten weeks, rather than eight.

At nine weeks, I stopped going to cardiac rehab, and I said good-bye to Amy and all the other cardiac nurses there. Knowing that I needed to return to work the following week, I wanted a break in between.

The cardiac nurses told me that I could now go to a regular gym and do similar exercises there. They cautioned me to use very low weights and to be careful not to strain my upper body. I hoped that once I returned to work, I would be able to keep up an active lifestyle and continue to get stronger.

The following weekend, I went back to a regular gym. However, without being hooked up to cardiac monitors, without anyone overseeing me, and with no cardiac nurses there to help if I was in trouble, I felt somewhat uneasy.

I cautiously used the machines that I was familiar with, keeping the speeds and the weights low, and I did mostly lower body work. For upper body, I reduced the weights to very little so that it did not feel strained at all, and I did only one or two sets of repetitions. It felt comfortable, and my fears started subsiding.

About that time, it also started sinking in how close I had come to dying. A few months earlier, I had had no idea what was wrong, and I had easily dismissed my symptoms, thinking I was just overweight and out of shape. Now I realized that without the surgery, I most likely would have died within one month, as so little oxygenated blood was getting through to the rest of my body.

It also hit me how easily I could have died in Hawaii, especially straining my body with all the walking we did, and specifically that day of the kayak trip, when I swam in the ocean. The thought of that humbled me and made me feel weak with gratitude for still being alive.

I figured that I must have some good guardian angels watching over me, and they must have been working overtime trying to keep me alive through all of that.

And maybe I had a strong will to live after all.

18

Returning to Routines

Going back to work was a little disconcerting. I was not yet quite ready for a full schedule, and I was not sure what would be expected of me. It still was somewhat uncomfortable driving, especially in rush-hour traffic, but I had no choice. And as eating continued to tire me, I also still needed to sleep after lunch.

On my first day back at work, I was greeted very warmly by the bosses and all my coworkers. I carried my red heart pillow with me, and I proudly showed my scar to everyone. I answered all their questions, and it felt comforting to be back in a familiar routine.

Sitting at my desk, I at first felt a bit out of it and not sure if I would remember everything that I needed to do. However, as I worked, it gradually came back to me, and I took my time, including cautiously walking to the mailbox.

One coworker, who had become a friend, offered to take me out to lunch, but I declined. I explained that I was still too exhausted and needed to rest and take a nap after lunch, and thankfully she understood.

After lunch that day, and every day following, I went out to my car, set an alarm to wake me up, and then dozed for about a half hour.

Each day at work, the job demands and routines became a little easier, and it wasn't long before I was back in the swing of things. However, I continued to take my time and work slowly, and all the tasks eventually got done, even if they were done a little bit slower than before.

I started going back to the gym on a regular basis, and the more I went, the more comfortable it felt. I was careful to keep the weight levels low on the machines so that I did not strain myself, but I did enough repetitions to get a decent workout.

In addition to the gym, at home I also continued doing my leg exercises, upper body stretches, a limited workout with weights similar to what I had been doing at rehab, and walking around the neighborhood. All of that helped me feel strong and assured me that I was on a continuing road to good health.

∽~∾

"Let's go for a walk," Dumitru said to me one mild Saturday afternoon in October.

"Great idea, I'd love to," I said, eagerly jumping up. We grabbed keys, left the house, and strolled up and down the streets in our neighborhood. Getting caught up in admiring the various houses and landscaping, we started rating the homes that we passed.

"This one gets two paws up," I quipped, my love of dogs mixing with my memory of the TV show that rated movies.

Dumitru pointed to the next house. "This one is three paws up and a tail wag."

Rating the homes and laughing, we easily covered over two miles before we got back to our house.

"You were walking fast," Dumitru told me after we returned home.

"I was?"

"Yes, I was impressed."

"Wow, I didn't even think about it. I was just enjoying the walk."

"That shows how much you've improved, and that you're still getting better."

"I guess that's true," I said. "I definitely feel much better now than I did before the surgery."

That weekend, I decided that I felt well enough to start socializing again, and we got together for dinner with our close friends, Diana and Brad, at our favorite local Italian restaurant. After being seated in a booth and ordering our food, the conversation turned to my surgery.

"How are you feeling now?" Diana asked me.

"Better," I told her. "It's a long process of recovery. I'm slowly healing and getting stronger, but it's taking a lot longer than I expected."

"That was a serious and invasive surgery," she told me. "So give yourself time to heal. The recovery will take a while."

"It's hard. Some days I feel strong and a lot better. And then other days, I still feel weak and it seems like I'll never feel better again."

The waiter placed a large bowl of salad on the table, and we helped ourselves.

"Recovery is never just a straight line of improvement," Diana told me. "There will always be good days and bad days."

"I know," I said, munching on my salad. "I just want to have it all over and feel good again."

"You will," she said gently. "Let the healing take its course. One day you will feel good again, I promise."

Our waiter arrived with steaming plates of food, and the tangy aroma of garlic and spices enveloped us.

"I am so thankful that you are my friends," I told them. "Sharing life, even the difficult times, with good friends really helps a lot."

"We feel the same way," Diana said.

A pressing need to cough started building, and I quickly grabbed my red heart pillow and pressed it firmly into my sternum as my body shook with coughing and I felt my face grimace with the strain.

"That looks really painful," Brad said.

"It is, coughing still really hurts," I told him, putting my pillow back down on the seat next to me. "And sneezing is much worse. But overall, it is slowly getting easier and less painful."

"Let us know if we can help with anything," Brad offered.

We shared stories and kind words with each other as we finished our meal. After dinner we walked out into the cool evening air, said good-bye, gently hugged each other, and promised to get together again soon.

For the next few months, I continued to improve. We started seeing a few more friends, and it felt good to keep up with our social connections.

I increased my walking to two miles at a time, and it began to feel like I was finally re-joining the human race.

19

CHICAGO

One year after the surgery, I went to Dr. Tillman's office for a check-up and echocardiogram.

"Your heart sounds great, and your echocardiogram is excellent. Everything looks good," Dr. Tillman told me after the exam and testing. "But I'm concerned about your weight." He looked at me sternly and then added, "If you put on too many more pounds, the valve won't fit right, and at some point it will not fit at all. You need to keep your weight down."

Dr. Tillman then said that he considered me healthy and that he only needed to see me for a check-up once every three years. It felt wonderful that he considered me that healthy, and also a little scary that I would not see any physician for three years. But I was glad to be returning to a more normal routine.

A few weeks later, in celebration of my one-year anniversary of the surgery, we decided to go on a much-needed vacation. We figured that I had healed enough to handle it, and we chose to go to Niagara Falls, with a quick stop first in Chicago to visit Daniel, Dumitru's childhood friend.

Dr. Soldano had warned me that there was a possibility that the metal holding my breastbone together might set off the metal detectors in airport security. I worried about that – *how would I explain to security personnel why the alarm was set off?*

We arrived at LAX airport, and as this was my first post-surgery flight, I felt a bit nervous as I approached airport security. *Would the wires in my chest set off the metal detectors?* Holding my hands up, I gingerly made my way through the x-ray machine, and I passed through without any alarm going off. *What a relief!* Since then I have flown many times, and I have never set off the alarm.

This time I was able to walk through the airport to our gate with no problem. There was no need to stop or rest, and I was actually walking pretty quickly – in fact, we were passing most other people, and that was so rewarding.

Feeling that it was too bulky for travel, and not wanting to risk losing it, I did not take my heart pillow with me, and I felt somewhat naked and vulnerable without it. I hoped that I would not regret that decision.

After arriving in Chicago, we rented a car and drove out to see Daniel. He lived in a suburb just north of the city and, with the help of GPS, we easily found his house with no problem. We parked in front of the contemporary two-story home and walked up to the front door.

"Hi, welcome, come in," Daniel warmly greeted us. After a friendly hug, the two guys laughed and joked with each other, and it was obvious that they immediately felt the joyful connection they had had since childhood. They gently kidded each other and caught up on the latest news, as they enjoyed a touching and heart-felt reunion.

Sharing homemade cookies with us that evening, Daniel offered to take us to downtown Chicago the next day, and we eagerly agreed.

The following morning was windy and cool, and we got off to an early start. After driving a few blocks and feeling the strong wind sway the car a few times, we left the car in a small parking lot and took the train downtown.

I carried a sweatshirt with me, and I discovered that I could roll it into a ball and use it in place of my heart pillow when I coughed. This worked very well, and it became my new security blanket on the trip.

Watching the passing scenery from the train windows while holding my sweatshirt, I looked forward to seeing all the sights in Chicago. Once we got off the train, Daniel pointed to buildings and explained what we were looking at, as we walked down the streets.

Happy and excited, and wearing new comfortable walking shoes, I wanted to walk fast, especially after sitting so long on the train. More interested in seeing the sights around us than hearing about them, I vaguely listened to Daniel, letting his words fade into the background. Looking around, I picked up the pace to a brisk walk, assuming that the guys were right behind me. At the end of the first block, I glanced back and saw that Dumitru and Daniel were about a half block back, slowly strolling along. I waited for them to catch up, and then I took off again.

Walking fast felt invigorating, and I loved strutting down the streets. However, I kept finding myself way ahead of the guys, and each time I looked back at them, Dumitru smiled at me and shrugged. I couldn't understand why they were walking so slowly.

We wandered over the waterways, captivated by the boats, and walked up and down many streets. Then we went to the top of the Sears Tower. Getting right up to the huge windows, we were amazed at the expansive views.

After coming back down, we again ambled along many streets, back over the waterways, walking well over five miles total. Beginning to tire, I finally slowed my pace and stayed with Dumitru and Daniel.

Before returning to the train station, we grabbed a quick lunch and relaxed for a bit. We then boarded the train and, after all that walking, it felt really good to sit down. Then from that small parking lot, we drove back to Daniel's house, as a light rain began to fall, sprinkling a fine mist on the windshield and the roads.

That evening, as the rain increased and pounded on the roof, Daniel's wife served us a delicious home-cooked dinner, which we thoroughly enjoyed. Daniel and his wife were warm, gracious, kind people, and we really cherished our time with them.

Later, as we were preparing for bed, Dumitru told me that Daniel had complained to him that I had been walking too fast. *What? Too fast? After recovering from open-heart surgery? Ha!* I took that as a huge compliment and confirmation of my progress, and it made me smile.

We drifted to sleep, listening to the rain splattering on the windows and hearing the deep booming thunder overhead.

20

Niagara Falls

The following day, we woke up to find that the storm had passed, and the air was now clean and brisk. After a hot breakfast, we said thank-you and good-bye to Daniel and his wife, and we drove back to the airport, returned our rental car, and made our way to our gate. We then flew from Chicago to Buffalo, New York.

In Buffalo we rented a car, crossed the border into Canada, and drove to the Hilton Hotel. Our room was on the top floor, and there was an enormous window. The dramatic view drew us in – our room overlooked both the American Falls and the Horseshoe Falls. The panorama was spectacular and mesmerizing and, for a long while, the view held us spellbound.

After unpacking, we couldn't wait to see Niagara Falls up close, and we walked roughly three-quarters of a mile to get there. The route to the Falls included walking down one street which was a steep slope, and I worried about being able to walk back up that street later on the return trip.

The power of Niagara Falls enveloped us, and we got as close as we could. It was thrilling and breathtaking, overwhelming all our senses, and we were astounded at the magnificence before us.

As it was already late afternoon, we stayed at the Falls for only about an hour, and we then headed back to the hotel. At the bottom of that steep uphill climb, I hesitated. *Could I do this?*

Then we started up, and I found that it was not too bad. About half-way up, we stopped to catch our breath, and then we continued the rest of the way to the top, crossed the street, and went into our hotel. Even with our one rest stop, it was easier than I had expected, and I was not winded or out of breath.

The next morning, filled with excitement, we walked back down the hill. We took a boat tour right up into the spray of the Falls and a walking tour of the Falls, and then we walked back up the hill to our hotel for lunch. I felt great – *what a thrill to be able to do all that!*

In the afternoon, we went to the hotel's indoor pool. This was the first time since my surgery that I would be seen in a bathing suit in public, and I was a bit nervous because my thick, red scar was very visible, protruding from the top of my bathing suit.

I worried that I might get kicked out of the pool if the lifeguards judged me as being either sick or as too great of a liability risk. But thankfully no one said anything, and we were able to enjoy the pool in peace.

There was a three-story slide into the pool, and we were excited to try it. However, to reach the top of the slide, we had to climb three flights of stairs. By the top flight, I was slowing down, but I made it.

The fast and thrilling trip down the curving slide, with a huge splash into the pool, was so much fun that we couldn't wait to do it again. We ended up climbing those stairs and joyfully flying down the slide at least a dozen times.

Each morning over the next three days we went on at least one of the many available tours – through the Falls, behind the Falls, walking around the Falls, and even in a boat through the whirlpool farther down the river. And every afternoon we played in the hotel pool and went down the slide, feeling like excited, happy kids having the best time.

The days passed quickly, and on our flight back home, we agreed that this was one of our favorite vacations. Looking back at what we did, I was absolutely amazed at all the walking, including hills and stairs, which I had done. After open-heart surgery one year earlier, I felt that I was now finally healed!

When we landed in Los Angeles, I quickly and easily walked the length of the airport, effortlessly passing other people with no problem. I felt strong and confident.

In addition, since my sweatshirt had been an excellent substitute for the red heart pillow, I realized that I no longer needed the pillow as a constant crutch.

21

Enjoying Life Again

A few weeks later, in August, we joined our friends at an event with the Sierra Club. We drove up to their lodge in Mt. Baldy, located in the local mountains just outside of Los Angeles. This was where Dumitru and I had first connected with each other thirteen years earlier, and we always loved going there.

This time I couldn't help but remember that "B-A-L-D-Y" was the word that I had spelled into Dumitru's hand when I had first come out of anesthesia after my surgery. Now this place felt magical to me.

At an elevation of 7,000 feet, the lodge was set off a curvy road filled with hairpin turns, in the middle of pine trees, clean fresh air, and many hiking trails. We were excited to be there, and we looked forward to hiking and connecting with friends.

We arrived at the lodge a little after noon, and we ran in to greet whoever might be there. Not everyone had gotten there yet, and we sat down in the dining room with the few people who had arrived earlier. Eating sandwiches and a salad, the lunch that we had brought with us, we talked with our friends, and I showed everyone my scar.

Once more friends arrived, a group of us put on hiking boots, grabbed bottles of water, and went for a hike in the local mountains. With backpacks on our backs, we headed out of the lodge and hiked two miles up a fairly steep hill, to where a dirt path led off to the left.

We turned onto the dirt path and hiked down a narrow rocky pathway to a beautiful waterfall. After talking, laughing, and enjoying the scenery and fresh air for about 30 minutes, we hiked back up to the main road and then headed back down the steep hill to the lodge.

Even with the high elevation, I was able to keep up with the group, and I was thrilled that I could do this hike. It was another validation of my recovery, of being healthy, and that the new heart valve was performing properly.

For well over a year, other than that one vacation to Chicago and Niagara Falls, I always kept my red heart pillow close to me, using it to help relieve the pain whenever I coughed or sneezed. It was close to two years before I put that heart pillow into a bag and stuffed it in the back of my closet.

Looking back over the entire medical and surgical journey, I now considered my scar to be a badge of honor, a testament to my difficult and dramatic recovery.

Filled with delight and wonder, and so grateful to be alive, I felt a deep sense of fulfillment. It felt incredibly good to be active again and doing the things I loved – hiking, working out, going on vacations, joining in on Sierra Club activities, and seeing friends. I treasured every moment and loved being energetic and healthy, something that I had almost lost.

But even more than that, there was a space of peace and joy that now infused everything. I did not ever again want to take for granted the amazing, awe-filled, profound experience of simply being alive, and having the incredible opportunity to walk upon this earth. The sights, sounds, smells, and feel of each moment filled me with astounding joy.

Finally feeling completely healed, I looked back over the entire experience, and I was proud of my journey. I was thrilled to again be part of humanity and part of life.

Now I felt much more in touch with the magnificent delight and elation that come from the endless and profound power of the life that surrounds us and fills us, permeating everything we do, everything we are, and everything there is.

I was filled with awe – and that has never left me. To this day, I find myself touching that space of peace and wonder, and I am filled with infinite happiness and gratitude.

Thankful and humbled to be alive, I now smile a lot more often, as I open to an incredibly beautiful place of deep peace and immense joy.

22

A Poem of Gratitude

Four months after my surgery, I had felt motivated to write a poem about my experience. Pleased with how it had come out, I sent copies of the poem, along with a heart-felt thank-you note, to Dr. Tillman, the cardiologist, and to Dr. Soldano, the cardiac surgeon.

Here I share with you a copy of my poem, which was written October 20, 2005.

Heart Surgery Poem

>I had been feeling short of breath,
>And uphills made me curse;
>I knew I'd have to get checked out
>'Cause it was getting worse.
>
>I went to see my doctor;
>It was just the very start
>Of tests that they would do to find
>The problem with my heart.

It couldn't just be fixed with pills
Or cream or even salve.
They had to cut me open and
Replace my aortic valve.

I trusted all my doctors there,
I heard they were the best.
I knew they'd do a super job
When cutting through my chest.

My condition was so very bad,
They waited just one day,
Then cut my chest and stopped my heart
And iced it right away.

They gave me a new tissue valve
And put it in somehow.
And then they sewed me up again
And then I was part cow.

I woke up in the ICU,
My husband by my side.
I was glad that it was over;
I could easily have died.

I had to cough and walk around
And eat to get some strength.
I took a peek at the scar I had,
It was one-half foot in length.

Coughing hurt but also helped,
The nurses did explain.
But I would hug my pillow tight
To help relieve the pain.

The first few days went by so fast,
I was in a kind-of haze.
And then I was released, and
I went home in just four days.

I was in shock and disbelief;
I was shaken to my core.
But I still coughed and ate and walked,
Each day a little more.

My husband helped me bathe and dress,
And even helped me eat.
He took amazing care of me,
Which was no easy feat.

I went to rehab, drove my car,
And slowly I felt stronger.
I cut back on my Advil, and
My walks kept getting longer.

Although my chest still hurts each day,
And movement makes it ache.
I'm much more independent now,
And I know what was at stake.

I've now been back at work two months,
Without a lot of strife.
And now each day, I still improve
And cherish my brand new life.

Copyright © 2005 Lynn Miclea

Epilogue

For the first few years after the procedure, I was preoccupied by, and very conscious of, having been through open-heart surgery. On a daily basis the signs of the surgery were obvious, and I could not escape it.

Each day when I dressed or undressed, I would see my thick, ropy scar in the mirror. And, for a very long time, it still hurt to cough or sneeze. These were constant daily reminders, and being a recipient of an artificial heart valve and a survivor of open-heart surgery became part of my identity.

Now in 2016, eleven years later, I often forget about the surgery although, out of habit, I still usually press back on my sternum when I sneeze. For the most part, I now go about life much more normally, but with an increased appreciation for still being here.

To this day, I often wake up each morning surprised, elated, ecstatic, and grateful to still be here on earth another day. *I am still alive – wow!*

Choosing the tissue valve was definitely a good decision for me, and I am very happy that I made that choice. I am glad that I have not been on Coumadin or on any blood thinners, other than a baby aspirin each evening. I know that in another eight-to-ten years, I will need another surgery to replace my current artificial heart valve. And at that time, I will get another tissue valve.

I remain very hopeful that medical knowledge and techniques will have advanced enough that I will not need another open-heart surgery. It will most likely be done through a small incision or through a catheter. Advancements in this area are already happening at a fast pace, so I am confident that the next surgery and the recovery will be much easier for me.

Although still struggling with my weight, I am eating healthier and continue to walk at least one mile every day, and I am glad that I remain more than 30 pounds less than I was at the time of my surgery in 2005.

❦

Over the first few months after the surgery, I started thinking whether there might possibly be metaphysical reasons for the faulty, stenotic heart valve.

Did I in any way somehow cause this? Was it a manifestation or reflection of my spiritual heart? Was my spiritual heart that closed? Was my heart, both physically and emotionally, constricted because I didn't feel that I deserved love? Did I feel so horribly unlovable? Was I too judgmental, critical, and unloving of others? Or did I not love myself? Was all of this a result of something that I needed to heal within myself, not just physically, but also emotionally and spiritually?

Since then, I have come to realize that I am a good person, worthy and deserving of love and life, as we *all* are. I understand that it was not yet my time to go, and I did not deserve to die.

I am also working at being more open-hearted, compassionate, and loving, both with others and with myself. So whether or not this physical condition was a manifestation or reflection of a metaphysical space, I really don't know – but in any case, it has helped me learn to open my spiritual heart and be more loving. And that process still continues today.

I will again face these issues when it's time for my next surgery to replace my current artificial heart valve with another one. And no matter how the next surgery will be done, I trust that I will be able to handle it and heal from it.

In the meantime, I am so very thankful to be alive and to still have a chance to continue to learn to be a better and more loving person, both with others and with myself.

∽~∾

I have come to realize that healing takes place on many levels, all of which are interconnected, even if we are not aware of it. This healing is needed for us to be whole – or actually, to realize that underneath the struggle, we already *are* whole.

What we mostly notice in our lives are the fragments – the thoughts, feelings, and interpretations from which we try to find meaning in our experiences and understand ourselves and the world. But sometimes when we stop trying so hard to understand, we can simply open to and become aware, with deep awe, of the life which surrounds and flows through us in each moment.

And in that space, we find peace. Underlying all our issues and difficulties, there is a place of serenity and tranquility where we discover our essence of pure consciousness, life, and love, and within which we are already whole.

I now understand that the more healing there is on multiple levels, the closer we get to touch that wholeness. Physical, mental, emotional, and spiritual – all are connected, as they overlap and merge into a magnificent, joyous totality of wholeness.

After all this, I am left with a sense of connection, unity, and oneness with all life, which fills me with joy and exuberance beyond words.

And I am so very grateful that I am still alive today. *Wow!*

Much love, peace, joy, and wholeness to each of you.

Lynn, the author, with Dumitru, her husband – 2015:

About the Author

LYNN MICLEA is a writer, author, editor, musician, Reiki master practitioner, and dog lover.

After retiring, Lynn further pursued her passion for writing, and she is now a successful author with many books published and more on the way.

She has written numerous short stories and published many books including thrillers, science fiction, paranormal, romance, mystery, memoirs, a grammar guide, self-help guided imagery, short story collections, and children's stories (fun animal stories about kindness, believing in yourself, and helping others).

She hopes that through her writing she can help empower others, stimulate people's imagination, and open new worlds as she entertains with powerful and heartfelt stories and helps educate people with her nonfiction books.

Originally from New York, Lynn currently lives in Southern California with her loving and supportive husband.

Please visit *www.lynnmiclea.com* for more information.

Books by Lynn Miclea

Fiction

New Contact

Transmutation

Journey Into Love

Ghostly Love

Guard Duty

Loving Guidance

The Diamond Murders

The Finger Murders

The Sticky-Note Murders

Short Story Collections

Beyond the Abyss – Science Fiction

Beyond Terror – Thrillers, Horror, and Suspense

Beyond Love – Love and Romance

Beyond Connections – Family and Relationships

Non-Fiction

Grammar Tips & Tools

Ruthie: A Family's Struggle with ALS

Mending a Heart: A Journey Through Open-Heart Surgery

Unleash Your Inner Joy – Volume 1: Peace

Unleash Your Inner Joy – Volume 2: Abundance

Unleash Your Inner Joy – Volume 3: Healing

Unleash Your Inner Joy – Volume 4: Spirituality

Children's Books

Penny Gains Confidence

Sammy and the Fire

Sammy Visits a Hospital

Sammy Meets Grandma

Sammy Goes to the Dog Park

Sammy Falls in Love

Sammy and the Earthquake

Sammy Goes On Vacation

Wish Fish: Book 1 – Discovering the Secret

Wish Fish: Book 2 – Endless Possibilities

ONE LAST THING...

Thank you for reading this book — I hope you loved it!

If you enjoyed this book, I'd be very grateful if you would post a short review on Amazon. Your support really makes a big difference and helps me immensely!

Simply click the "leave-a-review" link for this book at Amazon, and leave a short review. It would mean a lot to me!

Thank you so much for your support—it is very appreciated!

Thank You!

Made in the USA
Las Vegas, NV
12 August 2023